KALORAMA
TRIANGLE

KALORAMA
TRIANGLE

THE HISTORY OF A
CAPITAL NEIGHBORHOOD

STEPHEN A. HANSEN
FOREWORD BY MATTHEW B. GILMORE

Charleston   London

THE
History
PRESS

Published by The History Press
Charleston, SC 29403
www.historypress.net

Front cover: top: LOC, Prints and Photographs Division; *bottom:* by the author.
Back cover: top: author's collection;*bottom:* LOC, Prints and Photographs Division.

First published 2011

Manufactured in the United States

ISBN 978.1.60949.421.6

Library of Congress Cataloging-in-Publication Data
Hansen, Stephen A.
Kalorama Triangle : the history of a capital neighborhood / Stephen A. Hansen.
p. cm.
Includes bibliographical references and index.
ISBN 978-1-60949-421-6
1. Kalorama (Washington, D.C.)--History. 2. Neighborhoods--Washington (D.C.)--Case
studies. 3. Washington (D.C.)--History. 4. Kalorama (Washington, D.C.)--Economic
conditions. 5. Kalorama (Washington, D.C.)--Social conditions. 6. Economic development-
-Washington (D.C.)--History. 7. Social change--Washington (D.C.)--History. 8. Washington
(D.C.)--Economic conditions. 9. Washington (D.C.)--Social conditions. I. Title.
F202.K25H36 2011
975.3--dc23
2011033917

CONTENTS

CONTENTS

FOREWORD

Neighborhoods in the District of Columbia each have their own unique stories and history, which, woven together, make up the history of the nation's capital. Kalorama Triangle is a neighborhood that, to date, has been only cursorily documented, yet it deserves a much closer look, which Stephen Hansen has done.

As early as the 1850s, new neighborhoods began developing outside the capital city planned by George Washington and Peter Charles L'Enfant; across the Eastern Branch was Uniontown, and a ways above Boundary Street lay Mount Pleasant. Decades later, Kalorama Triangle was seen as desirable when a whole complex of economic forces and real estate development pressures jostled in the post–Governor Shepherd era. Nearby Dupont Circle to the south became a fashionable neighborhood post–Civil War, and soon the District faced pressure to rationalize development even farther north—above Boundary Street and throughout Washington County. Plans had been drawn for the extension of Massachusetts Avenue, followed by controversy over extending Connecticut Avenue. Here many factors collided—District and federal government and private real estate developers (who sometimes also served as District officials or may have been federal officials). This critical area was the intersection of much larger external forces as various parties struggled to define the best way to push development all the way to the District's northern boundary and develop the connection to downtown proper. The extension of Connecticut bisected the hilly land of the Kalorama estate and Widow's Mite lands above Boundary Street (Florida Avenue), and ultimately what had started as Washington Heights developed into several neighborhoods: Washington Heights, Kalorama Triangle, Sheridan Kalorama (recognized as historic districts) and Adams Morgan.

In what follows, Hansen brings to life the development of Kalorama Triangle, drawing together the many disparate threads of the story, recalling many people whose names have faded from popular memory but were critical to the development of late nineteenth-century Washington. Kalorama Triangle was not developed by any single individual or as a singular neighborhood but, rather, was developed out of a crazy quilt of subdivisions. Hansen's approach is to review each subdivision—who laid it out and how it developed—not quite a block-by-block telling of the story but nearly. Hansen draws on almost two decades of historic preservation and archaeology experience, bringing together an impressive amount of detail about persons and places, biographical and architectural, with a trove of illustrations. This will be an invaluable addition to the bookshelf of anyone interested in the history of Washington, D.C. Hansen's story places Kalorama Triangle in its historical context as a key location in the city's development with a story having significance well beyond the boundaries of the neighborhood.

Matthew B. Gilmore
Editor, H-DC

ACKNOWLEDGEMENTS

This book would not have been possible without the assistance of Matthew B. Gilmore. Matthew has authored several books and articles on the history of Washington, D.C.; is the founding editor of H-DC, the Washington, D.C. history discussion website (www.h-net.org/~dclist); and serves on the editorial board of *Washington History*, the journal of the Historical Society of Washington, D.C. Matthew shared his expertise on the city's history, assisted in researching Kalorama Triangle's subdivisions, created the maps for use in the book and provided overall support throughout the project. I am also indebted to the staffs of the Washingtoniana Room at the Martin Luther King Library and the Library of Congress's Prints and Photographs Room, who were invaluable in helping to locate and assemble the photographs for this book. I would like to extend special thanks to Krista Kendall and Steven Lane, who were kind enough to review this book and provide comments, and to Eric Crabtree, whose keen interest and perspective helped to tell this story. I would like to dedicate this book to a dear friend, Richard Pierre Claude (1934–2011), who more than anyone taught me the importance of the written word in sharing knowledge and whose interest in this book was the impetus for its completion.

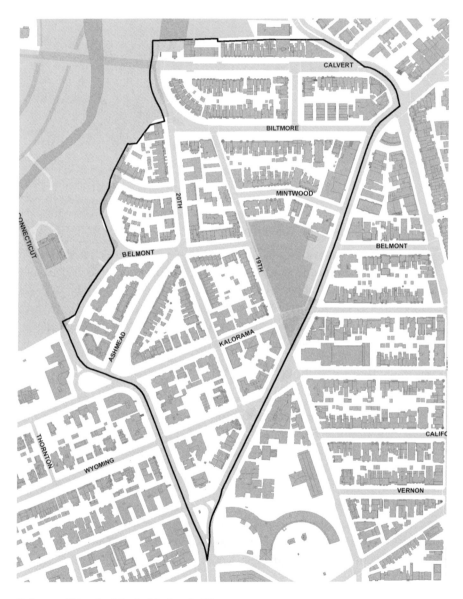

Kalorama Triangle. *Map by Matthew B. Gilmore.*

INTRODUCTION

The Kalorama Triangle neighborhood in Washington, D.C., is located in the northwest quadrant of the city, between Connecticut Avenue and Rock Creek Park to the west, Columbia Road to the east and Calvert Street to the north. It derives its name from the eighteenth-century Kalorama estate that was once located in the bordering Sheridan-Kalorama neighborhood. The name Kalorama Triangle was unofficially adopted in the 1960s during the urban renewal movement and became established when it became a nationally recognized historic district in 1987.

The Kalorama Triangle of today is much more than meets the eye, with layers of history that are not easily visible by simply walking down its streets or even by moving into the neighborhood itself. Residents live amid an invisible history—people who are long forgotten and buildings and communities that no longer exist. In previous times, residents might have known their neighborhood's history, having grown up as part of its community. But the history of this neighborhood quickly became lost in the transient character of modern Washington, D.C. While this book is an attempt to tell the untold story of creating one small place, it also brings to life familiar themes of American history spanning over three centuries.

The modern neighborhood of Kalorama Triangle in Washington, D.C., has its origins in a land grant in the seventeenth century. By the end of the Civil War, it remained rural hinterland to the city of Washington, home to only two farms. Yet the period up to the end of the Civil War was not uneventful, as Kalorama Triangle had already experienced much characterizing the development of the American colonies—a fatal Indian attack on its second owner, a son cheated out of his inheritance and slavery. The city of Washington began to grow beyond its original 1800 boundaries in the 1880s, with wealthy and ambitious landowners, developers and congressmen all transforming Kalorama Triangle from rural farmland to the national capital's first suburb in the short time span of about thirty years. The era following the Civil War witnessed the Industrial Revolution, the rise of real estate tycoons, the Gilded Age of the late nineteenth century and, in the twentieth century, the burgeoning of an urban middle class, followed by urban decline and then renewal. All this is reflected in the one small neighborhood of Kalorama Triangle.

This is also the story of the power of environment. While Kalorama Triangle today appears to be a single, integrated neighborhood, the diverse character of its original subdivisions or developments began to emerge when roads and house lots were carved out of farmland, laying the foundation for distinct micro socioeconomic environments. These environments reflected the ambitions and statuses of their developers and residents. House lots and home sizes affected degrees of social interaction within that particular environment—large individual mansions with spacious yards and walls offered less social intimacy than tightly clustered row houses, and both of these experiences were different from life in a grand apartment building.

These artificially created environments then attracted their intended occupants. The wealthy were the first to migrate, attracted to the larger lots on the verdant hills above the city, selecting prominent architects to create freestanding homes. Others would build grand town houses or choose to live in one of the new luxury apartment buildings. Some would purchase more modest town houses built on speculation, sitting shoulder to shoulder on narrower lots. Others of perhaps lesser means, but still desiring to be in a good location, would rent in one of the family-friendly apartment buildings that were beginning to fill urban spaces in the 1920s.

Starting with the Great Depression, as in most urban areas, Kalorama Triangle's population began to change. The modest rows of town houses, originally built on speculation for a professional set, became occupied by the working class, who began filling the gap created by the great migrations of the middle class to the suburbs. Many mid-size town houses were divided up into apartments or became boardinghouses. However, the luxurious apartment houses remained havens for the wealthy, offering a sense of separation from the changing demographics below. In addition, grand freestanding houses and elegant town houses continued to retain those with means to keep them intact. These were often embassies, social clubs, organizations and even churches.

During the urban renewal movement of the 1960s and '70s, Kalorama Triangle residents began to restore its legacy. The once luxurious apartment buildings became co-ops, reestablishing their status in the neighborhood. While modest town houses remained single-family homes throughout, their ownership gradually returned to the professional urban class. Many of the larger town houses that had been boardinghouses were converted back to single-family residences. Others remained apartments and later were returned to their original elegance in the form of renovated condominiums.

Kalorama Triangle's subtle power of place has almost as much of an effect on its present residents as it did on its first occupants over one hundred years ago. New residents in many ways are attracted to and perhaps unknowingly adapt to an urban and social landscape that was planned and established before the turn of the twentieth century. While Kalorama Triangle is a relatively small place, hopefully the wider relevance of the history of this forty-acre parcel of land, from colonial Maryland to the present day, might help inspire all of us to learn more about what once existed in the places we now live.

THE ORIGINS OF KALORAMA TRIANGLE

Kalorama Triangle is located on a 670-acre seventeenth-century tract of land named the Widow's Mite and on a small part of a 1702 parcel of land called Pretty Prospect, much of which later became Georgetown in 1751. Until Washington was selected as the site for the nation's capital, the land that makes up Kalorama Triangle was part of Charles County, Maryland. In 1696, it was part of Prince George's County, created from part of Charles County, and then became part of the District of Columbia's Washington County in 1790.

LEGEND OF THE WIDOW'S MITE AND THE TREATY OAK

Many American cities have their share of legends and stories that tell of their founding. One of the famous legends regarding the settling of Washington, D.C. (and, more specifically, Kalorama Triangle) is that of the Widow's Mite. The legend tells that before Washington was occupied by white men, it was a vast forest occupied by the Anacostia tribe of Indians. Mannacasset, chief of the Anacostia, selected a site for his wigwam near a young and powerful oak tree on a prominence that provided a view of the surrounding country.

Two early European settlers taken captive by Mannacasset were a young mother and her daughter. When the mother refused to become his wife, the chief spared her life and that of her young daughter but decreed that the mother could never wander beyond the shade of the oak tree. Shortly after Mannacasset's death, George Washington selected this land for the site of the new national capital, and the treaty for its purchase was signed with the Indians under this great oak.

The mother was offered several homes but chose to remain under the great oak tree that had become her home. She was granted the tract of land consisting of seventeen and a half acres where the oak tree stood. The widow refused to sell the land when the hill site was being considered for the U.S. Capitol building but instead willed it to her daughter, with a request that the oak tree be regarded as a special relic in remembrance of the shelter it had provided her over the years.[1]

As with many legends, there are often truths that form the basis of the story but have been added to or combined with other stories after generations of retelling. In fact, in seventeenth-century Maryland, there was a widow with small children who was attacked by Indians. Along with the widow, two children survived the attack, one a girl. Of the two children killed in the attack, one had inherited a tract of land later to be called the Widow's Mite. The crest of the hill in Widow's Mite *does* provide a panoramic view over the city, and George Washington *was* asked to consider part of Widow's Mite as the site for the new capital.

The only treaty with the Indians in the area was made in 1652 with the Susquehannocks, who were warring with the settlers and Indians of the lower Potomac and Patuxent River regions twelve years before the tract of land called Widow's Mite was patented. In 1820, a small Federal-style house, Oak Lawn, was erected on a hill on Widow's Mite where a mighty oak tree stood. The house was razed in 1952. The following year, the four-hundred-year-old Treaty Oak, which stood only a few yards from the house, was cut down by real estate developers. This is now the site of the Washington Hilton Hotel.

There has been much speculation as to the true origin of the name "Widow's Mite." Many land grants had whimsical or playful names, often sounding more like the names of racehorses than tracts of land: Good Chance, Trouble Enough, the World's End and Expense, to name but a few. The most probable origin for the name of Widow's Mite is biblical and comes from Mark 12:42: "And there came a certain poor widow, and she threw in two mites, which make a farthing."

THE FIRST PROPRIETORS

THE LANGWORTHS AND WIDOW'S MITE

Maryland's earliest settlers were rugged and independent individuals. They were willing to depart England, often leaving their entire families behind, to indenture themselves for years for the price of passage in hopes of acquiring a piece of land that they could call their own and where they could perhaps derive an income from growing tobacco.

One of the earliest pioneers to Maryland was James Langworth. He was born in Kent, England, and was transported to Maryland in 1635 as an indentured servant.[2] Two years later, his brother John Langworth was transported to Maryland by Thomas Girrard.[3] James settled in St. Mary's City and then Charles County and served as captain of the provincial government's military company, as a member of the Lower House of Maryland and as a court justice.[4]

Although it did not receive its name until 1664, the first probable mention of Widow's Mite, the land grant upon which Kalorama Triangle now sits, was in the 1660 will of James Langworth, in which he left his son John 670 acres that were "yet to be taken up."[5] The specific language in Langworth's will suggests that what he left his son was a warrant, or the right to survey and claim a specified amount of acreage, which he had acquired sometime prior to his death. A patent, or title to the land, would be issued once the survey was completed and filed.

Widow's Mite was surveyed in 1664 for young John Langworth. While it might appear out of the ordinary for a survey to be conducted for a minor, it was not conducted for the other John Langworth, James's brother. James Langworth did not convey any land to his brother, who had already died by 1646 and who left his estate to his wife, were she to ever immigrate to Maryland.[6]

Determining the exact location and boundaries of the earliest land grants and titles can prove difficult. Generally, the southern part of Widow's Mite began in Foggy Bottom around Twenty-fourth and E Streets NW, the site of the future National Observatory. It extended northward along approximately Nineteenth Street to Florida Avenue, above which it expanded east to Seventeenth Street, west to Rock Creek and north to approximately Adams Mill Road.

INDIAN TROUBLES

The English-Indian conflict in the region was at its height at the time of James Langworth's death in 1660. Hostile encounters took the form not only of battles between groups of Indians and settlers but also of sporadic Indian raids on individual plantations and outlying settlements.

To protect against Indian attacks, the Maryland provincial government established companies of rangers to patrol the frontier and warn settlers of Indian movements. By the time of the founding of Prince George's County in 1696, these rangers patrolled the area beyond the Anacostia River, as far north as Sugarloaf Mountain in Frederick County and eastward toward Baltimore County.

In 1665, James Langworth's widow, Agatha, who was living in St. John, Charles County, Maryland, was lying ill at her house when four Mattawoman Indian men burst through the front door. Three of these men Agatha knew by name: Maquamps (known by the settlers as Bennett), Chotike and Inuoyce ("the old fisherman"). Chotike attacked Agatha with his tomahawk but was chased out of the house by a dog. The men then went through an orchard and cornfield, where they found Agatha's servant Elizabeth Brumley tending to the Langworth children. Agatha flung open a window and cried, "Indians, Indians!" while she heard her children saying, "Good nindians, good nindians." Brumley tried to quiet the children, but Maquamps decapitated "Jonny." Brumley fled with a girl, but Bennett followed her with the boy's head under his arm. He laid down the boy's head and struck her about the head with his tomahawk. Jonny and one other child were dead, and Brumley was left for dead. Bennett and another Indian were captured and tried, found guilty and sentenced to hang. The others were never captured.[7]

With the murder of young John Langworth, ownership of Widow's Mite passed to his brother William, who obtained the patent for it in 1681.[8] William died in 1693, leaving no male heirs to inherit his property. In his will, he stipulated that Widow's Mite was to be sold.[9]

THOMAS FLETCHALL

In 1714, the daughters of William Langworth, Elizabeth Hagan and Mary Routhorn, sold Widow's Mite to Thomas Fletchall for twelve thousand pounds of tobacco.[10] Thomas Fletchall was born in Scotland in 1657 and was a tobacco farmer in Prince George's County, Maryland. Fletchall had served with the Maryland Rangers under the command of Colonel Ninian Beall, as well as two terms as constable in 1705 and 1707. Prior to acquiring Widow's Mite, Fletchall had already amassed thousands of acres of land in and around Washington.

Fletchall had only owned Widow's Mite for three years before his death in 1717. In his will, Fletchall left half of Widow's Mite, a total of three hundred acres, to his son Thomas, to be given to him when he reached the age of twenty-one. To his wife, Ann, whom he also named executrix of his will, he left a dwelling house. And while not specifically naming Widow's Mite, he also left her three hundred acres adjacent to the plantation, which were to pass to his son Thomas upon her death.[11] The mention of a dwelling in his will suggests that Fletchall may have been the first settler to actually occupy Widow's Mite. The house may have been near a stream known as Slash Run, near present-day Nineteenth and M Streets NW.[12]

Fletchall's choice of where to divide Widow's Mite was probably determined by the fall line where the piedmont meets the coastal flat plain and where the terrain cedes to the rise of the hill near Florida and Connecticut Avenues today. The southern portion was prime land for tobacco farming and later became the object of real estate speculation when the land was deeded to the government in the 1790s for the new location of the nation's capital. The more rugged northern portion was to remain outside the city for decades and would become the future site of Kalorama Triangle.

As the executrix of her husband's will, Ann Fletchall was authorized to "sell several parcels of land" to pay any of Thomas's remaining debts.[13] The sale of two tracts of land—Charles and Thomas—the same year he died might indeed have been to satisfy those debts, but Ann did not limit sales to just several parcels. Within two years of Fletchall's death, Ann had married William Renshaw, a brick layer from Prince George's County who was also a witness to her husband's will. Along with Renshaw, Ann continued selling off Fletchall's vast holdings, including the six-hundred-acre tract of land falling within the federal city called the Gleaning,[14] which was to become the future site of the White House.

While she could not have foreseen the coming land speculation of the 1790s, Ann probably knew that the southern half of Widow's Mite was the most valuable for tobacco farming. By the time Thomas Jr. came of age, the southern half of Widow's Mite had been almost completely sold off. In 1723, after Ann Fletchall died, William Renshaw sold to Thomas the remaining 124 acres of her half of Widow's Mite (which he was actually due to inherit) for five pounds sterling.

When the younger Fletchall finally came into what was left of his inheritance in the northern part of Widow's Mite, it was not suitable for tobacco farming. In 1727, Thomas Fletchall sold the northern remains of Widow's Mite, now consisting of only 206 acres yet encompassing nearly all of modern-day Kalorama Triangle, to Anthony Holmead. By this time, young Thomas was living in Frederick County, Maryland, and was known there as "Poor Thomas."[15]

The Holmeads

Anthony Holmead, like Thomas Fletchall Sr., was a tobacco farmer from Prince George's County. And like Fletchall, he set out to acquire as much land as he possibly could, but not necessarily for tobacco farming. In 1765, he purchased two large tracts of land just north of Widow's Mite, Beall's Plains and Lamar's Outlet. He started to build his house, Holmead Manor, at the present-day location of the 3500 block of Thirteenth Street NW probably not long after he purchased Widow's Mite.

Without an heir, Anthony Holmead left his vast landholdings to his namesake nephew in 1750. The younger Anthony was born in Devon, England, in 1724. Like his uncle, Anthony continued to add to his vast real estate holdings, purchasing additional tracts of land around Rock Creek. Instead of taking up residence at the Holmead Manor house, in 1750 Anthony Holmead constructed a new house closer to Georgetown on the western part of the Holmead property with a view of the Potomac and Rock Creek. The house was located on the south side of the 2300 block of S Street NW.

THE NEW CAPITAL AND LAND SPECULATION

The Residence Act of 1790 gave President George Washington the authority to select a location along the Potomac for the nation's new capital. It also gave him the authority to appoint a surveyor and establish a three-man commission that, along with himself and Thomas Jefferson, would oversee the surveying of the federal district and have suitable buildings ready for Congress and other government offices by the first Monday in December 1800. The federal government would provide financing for the public buildings from profits generated by buying lots cheaply and selling or auctioning them at a higher price.

Robert Peter, along with other Georgetown merchants, suggested that the site of the proposed federal city be located on the land opposite Georgetown across Rock Creek, where he and Holmead owned hundreds of acres. This

Washington City, Georgetown and Washington County. The future location of Kalorama Triangle fell just outside Washington City to the northwest. *T.G. Bradford, 1835. Courtesy Library of Congress, Prints and Photographs Division.*

would have placed Washington City (the federal city) in present-day Kalorama Triangle. Unlike the land that ultimately would be chosen for the new capital, the proposed site comprised both flat and hilly terrain and was close enough to Georgetown that land would sell easily. George Washington ultimately selected the site spanning the plateau between the Potomac and the Eastern Branch Rivers. The District of Columbia Organic Act of 1801 incorporated the District of Columbia and divided the territory not designated for Washington City into two counties. Land ceded to the District from Prince George's County to the north and east of the Potomac River (which included Kalorama Triangle) became Washington County. Land ceded by Virginia to the west of the Potomac River became Alexandria County. Georgetown and Alexandria remained independent cities. The future location of Kalorama Triangle fell just outside Washington City to the northwest.

Expectations for the development of Washington City as an urban center spurred speculation that land in adjacent Washington County would increase in value, prompting a number of land resurveys and transactions west of Rock Creek in the 1790s.

In 1791, Holmead had Beall's Plains and Lamar's Outlet north of Widow's Mite resurveyed and combined under the name Pleasant Plains, the present-day location of the Mount Pleasant neighborhood. The following year, Robert Peter combined Plain Dealing with his other tracts of land immediately to the east of Window's Mite under the name Mount Pleasant. Peter's new Mount Pleasant patent was bordered by T Street to the south, Euclid Street to the north and Eighteenth Street to the west and is where the Washington Heights neighborhood is now located.

In 1794, Holmead subdivided part of Widow's Mite, carving out for himself a separate fifty-six-acre estate a little farther north of his first house, where he built a new house called Rock Hill,[16] now the site of Mitchell Park. That same year, Holmead sold about thirty acres, along with his first house, to District commissioner Gustavus Scott, who renamed the property Belair.

Gustavus Scott died penniless as a result of speculating on new house lots in Washington City. His widow sold Belair to William Augustine Washington, a nephew of George Washington, who in 1807 sold it to poet and diplomat Joel Barlow. Barlow thought that the name Belair for an estate was overused in Maryland and Virginia and changed its name to Kalorama, from the Greek meaning "fine view." The name continued to be associated with the estate until the 1880s, when it was subdivided into urban lots, and is the origin of the names of the Kalorama Triangle and Sheridan-Kalorama neighborhoods today.

Above: About 1795, Anthony Holmead constructed a new house named Rock Hill on the location of present-day Mitchell Park on S and Twenty-third Streets. Photo circa 1909. *Courtesy Library of Congress, Prints and Photographs Division.*

Below: The Kalorama estate after the fire of 1865. Originally built by Anthony Holmead and renamed Kalorama from Greek meaning "fine view" by Joel Barlow, it is the namesake of the Kalorama Triangle and Sheridan-Kalorama neighborhoods today. *Courtesy Library of Congress, Prints and Photographs Division.*

When Anthony Holmead died in 1802, he left his property to his wife, Susanna, his sons John and Anthony and his daughters Sarah Speak and Loveday Buchannon. Widow's Mite was divided among all his children. In 1805, Loveday married German immigrant and real estate broker Thomas W. Pairo. She eventually acquired Rock Hill and lived there until her death in 1852.

Colonel George Bomford bought the Kalorama estate from Joel Barlow in 1822 and gradually built the estate up to ninety acres. Bomford had served as chief of ordnance of the United States Army in the War of 1812. Like Gustavus Scott and so many proprietors at that time, Bomford became heavily involved in real estate speculation, and sometime before 1826, he had also acquired the Cliffbourne estate in Kalorama Triangle. By 1846, he was in such financial trouble that he was forced to sell both the Kalorama and Cliffbourne estates.

During the Civil War, the Kalorama mansion was commandeered by the U.S. Army for use as a smallpox hospital. During a gala ball on Christmas Eve 1865 to celebrate the army's departure, the east wing caught fire, killing many of the party's attendees.

KALORAMA TRIANGLE IN THE NINETEENTH CENTURY

COLUMBIA ROAD:
THE FIRST ROAD IN KALORAMA TRIANGLE

Colonel John Tayloe was a wealthy Virginian and builder of the Octagon House in Foggy Bottom at Eighteenth and New York Avenues, which was designed by Dr. William Thornton in 1800. Tayloe was an avid horse racing enthusiast and thoroughbred horse owner. In 1802, only two years after Congress arrived in Washington, Tayloe capitalized on the city's lust for horse racing and leased land from Anthony Holmead in Pleasant Plains to open the city's second racetrack. The first track was walking distance from the White House, where the Organization of American States is located today on Constitution Avenue NW. This first racetrack was so popular that Congress would recess to make post time at the track.

Columbia Road—also known by such names as the "road to Georgetown," "Rock Creek Road" and "County Road"—was often referred to in the nineteenth century as "Taylor Lane." That name may have been a corruption of Tayloe's Road or Tayloe's Lane, as it was the road to Tayloe's racetrack at the time.

Tayloe's racetrack was a one-mile oval centered on what is Fourteenth Street and Meridian Hill today, and it became a Washington institution. In 1822, a reputed ten thousand people at the track watched a horse named Eclipse win a $5,000 stake where a large amount of money changed hands.[17]

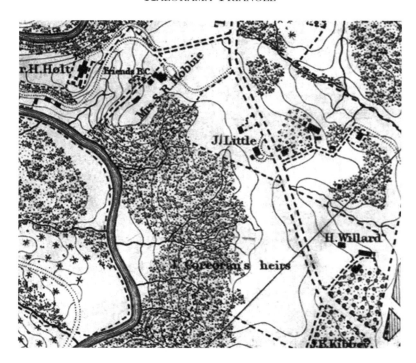

Landowners and property lines in Kalorama Triangle in the late 1850s. At this time, the land in Kalorama Triangle was owned by only three individuals: the Corcoran heirs, John Little and Mrs. S.R. Hobbie. The house shown belonging to Mrs. S.R. Hobbie was Cliffbourne, the first house built in Kalorama Triangle. *Albert Boschke's "Topographical Map of the District of Columbia" (1861). Courtesy Library of Congress, Prints and Photographs Division.*

The track operated until about 1840 as the National Jockey Club under the ownership of John Maddox, former groomsman and horse trainer for the Oglethorps and William Thornton, among others. In 1845, William Holmead subdivided the track into lots for sale for building country residences. Columbia Road's name remains from the time when it was the road to Columbia College, which was later built on the site of Tayloe's racetrack. Columbia College later became George Washington University and moved to its present location in Foggy Bottom.

THE FIRST HOUSE IN KALORAMA TRIANGLE

The first house built in Kalorama Triangle stood on the west side of present-day Cliffbourne Place, between Calvert and Biltmore Streets. It would give its name to a Civil War barracks and hospital, an 1898 subdivision and the street itself. The first documented appearance of the Cliffbourne house is on an 1861 map of Washington, D.C., created by Albert Boschke and surveyed in the late 1850s that shows a large estate immediately to the north of the Little farm belonging to Mrs. S.R. Hobbie. The house was approached by a long drive from Columbia Road terminating in a circle at the front of the house, similar to large country estates in Virginia and Maryland. To date, the history of this house prior to and after its ownership by Mrs. Hobbie has been overlooked. The first resident of this house was most likely the first person to live in Kalorama Triangle.

When William Thornton acquired land for his horse farm in Kalorama Triangle from John Holmead and Thomas Peter in 1815, both deeds referenced an earlier adjacent property owned by John Holmead and Thomas W. Pairo. When Loveday Buckhannon married Thomas Pairo in 1805, it is likely that the couple wanted land and a house of their own and that Loveday carved out the northern part of Widow's Mite for herself and her husband. As was common with early nineteenth-century property rights, her inherited share of Widow's Mite would have remained in one of her brothers' names until a title could be transferred to her husband.

Cliffbourne, literally meaning "bordering on a cliff," was an appropriate name for the estate—it sat on the crest of a tract of land that ended at a steep bluff where it met the Rock Creek Valley to the west.

The Pairos ultimately returned to the Holmeads' Rock Hill home. The Cliffbourne estate came into the hands of Rock Hill neighbor, Kalorama estate owner and real estate speculator Colonel George Bomford. In 1826, Bomford placed Cliffbourne in trust as collateral to Richard Smith in order to secure a loan from the Bank of the United States.[18] By 1837, a financially strapped Bomford had failed to repay the loan, entitling Richard Smith to sell the property to cover the debt. But Smith did not sell Cliffbourne right away. He was probably occupying the house and had no intentions of leaving. The property briefly returned to the Holmeads in 1845 when Richard Smith finally sold it to Charles Hedges James,[19] who had married Mary Ellen Holmead. The next year, James sold Cliffbourne to Selah Reeve Hobbie,[20] a former congressman from New York who also served as first assistant postmaster general. Almost immediately, Hobbie leased the property back to Richard Smith.[21]

George Bomford never recovered from his losses and died of a broken heart in a modest house on I Street NW in 1848.[22] Selah Hobbie died in 1854, and his widow, Julianne, would move to Cliffbourne after the Civil War. The house stood until 1899, when it was razed for homes in the new Cliffbourne subdivision.

DR. WILLIAM THORNTON

Dr. William Thornton was born in Tortola in the British Virgin Islands in 1759 and received his early training as a physician. He was also an inventor, painter, poet and amateur architect. He is probably best known as the original designer of the Capitol building. Thornton served as the first architect of the Capitol and was appointed by George Washington as a city commissioner and as the first superintendent of the United States Patent Office by Thomas Jefferson. Thornton is credited for single-handedly saving the patent office during the British siege of Washington in 1814 by comparing it to the great library at Alexandria to the British soldiers outside with torches in their hands. This had the desired effect.

Dr. William Thornton, the first architect of the Capitol, bought farmland in Kalorama Triangle from the Holmead and the Peter families for a horse farm. *Courtesy D.C. Public Library Commons.*

In 1815, Dr. William Thornton wanted land in Kalorama Triangle. With the land in Washington City divided into single house lots, it was a good investment, provided ample grazing land for his horses and was close to Tayloe's racetrack. In 1815, Robert Peter's son Thomas deeded Thornton 22½ acres of his father's former Mount Pleasant tract, and in 1817, John Holmead deeded to Thornton 33¾ acres of Widow's Mite.[23] Thornton never lived on the property himself, as it was easily accessible by horse from his home in Georgetown. When Thornton died in 1828, his widow, Anna Maria, sold the property to Christian and Matthew Hines.

CHRISTIAN AND MATTHEW HINES

Christian and Matthew Hines were the sons of Johannes Heintz, a German immigrant and Revolutionary War veteran, and were born near Liberty in Frederick County, Maryland. Christian was born in 1781, and he and his brother stayed in Frederick County until 1790, when they resettled with their parents in Georgetown.

During the War of 1812, Christian Hines was a member of Richard S. Briscoe's Company of Militia, which was attached to the First Legion in the City of Washington and fought in the Battle of Bladensburg. In 1814, Christian met and shared a glass of wine with Pierre Charles L'Enfant, the designer of the plan of the federal capital.[24]

The Hines brothers had a grocery store in Foggy Bottom at the southwest corner of Twentieth and I Streets NW. They later opened a furniture store at 822 Twentieth Street NW. Matthew Hines died in 1862, and Christian continued the business alone until his death in 1874. His funeral took place in the furniture store.

When the Hines brothers bought the land from Anna Maria Thornton in 1828, they planned to cultivate silkworms on the property and planted a number of mulberry trees. On the southeast corner of where Belmont Road now meets Columbia Road, they built a modest one-and-a-half-story, twenty-five-square-foot house. *Sunday Star* correspondent John Clagett Proctor, writing in 1940, said that he remembered the whitewashed house in this youth.[25] The house was destroyed by fire in the late 1880s and is now the site of the Norwood apartment building at 1868 Columbia Road.

Christian Hines and his brother Matthew bought William Thornton's property in Kalorama Triangle in 1828 to cultivate silkworms. *In Proctor, "Christian Hines."*

The silkworm industry proved unprofitable, and the loss of a $900 investment in the Potomac Canal Company ruined the Hines brothers. They defaulted on their mortgage, and in 1836, the property was deeded to John Little.

Some members of the Hines family were buried in the northern part of their land. The burial plot was located at the corner of Columbia Road and Eighteenth Street, in the rear of stores now at 2440–2444 Eighteenth Street. In 1915, Margaret Foyle Sands, daughter of the next owner of the property, John Little, responded to an inquiry as to the location of the graves. From her home in the Mendota apartment building, she wrote:

> *The burying ground you spoke of was in an oak grove not far from the old pear trees and on the same side of the street, there are no trees left and every trace of the graves gone. There was never a stone to mark any of the graves. I only remember hearing my parents say that the Hines' were buried there. It was used for a burial place for our family servants and I think my mother had two very young children buried there. The place is entirely built over by small stores on 18th St.*[26]

It is quite probable that the "servants" Margaret Sands referred to were some of the Littles' slaves.

JOHN LITTLE'S FARM

John Little, an Irish immigrant, was born in 1805 and became a successful butcher and farmer. Little had a butcher stand at the Center Market located at Seventh Street and Pennsylvania Avenue NW, now the site of the National Archives. He also maintained an abattoir or slaughterhouse built into the hillside between what is now Champlain and Eighteenth Streets, about a block or two north of Florida Avenue where Slash Run once flowed. At the time he purchased the Hineses' farm, he may have occupied the modest house constructed by the Hineses on the property.

From the time he purchased the property from the Hines brothers, the size of his household, slaveholdings and personal property continued to grow. The 1850 census for the household included his wife, Margaret, and his five daughters: Sarah, Finnella, Sophia, Margaret and Ida. In addition to the family members, the census also shows that Little had four laborers living in his household: a white male farmer, two black male laborers and a thirty-two-year-old black woman. In 1855, John Little's brother Samuel died and left John as guardian of his nephew and niece, John O. and Julia A. Little.

The John Little house was located on the site of Kalorama Park. In 1862, Little had twelve slaves in his possession, and family members had a couple more. Photo circa 1920. *Courtesy the Historical Society of Washington, D.C.*

Needing more room for his growing household, John Little built a large three-story dwelling on his land on the opposite side of Columbia Road in the 1850s, now the location of Kalorama Park. And his household continued to grow. By 1860, twenty-seven individuals were listed in the Little household. John Little's sisters, Eliza and Maria Little, had also come to live with him.

By 1861, there were a total of seventeen enslaved African Americans living on John Little's farm, twelve owned by Little himself and five by his niece and nephew.[27] By now, Little had three buildings on the west side of Taylor Lane (Columbia Road): the manor house, a carriage house directly west of the manor and a third house just to the north of the manor. There were also six buildings on the east side of Taylor Lane where Little had his cattle farm and slaughterhouses.

The 1862 Compensated Emancipation Act provided compensation for each slave formerly owned by loyal Unionist masters. When Little filed his Petition for Compensation by the District of Columbia in 1862, he indicated that he had twelve slaves in his possession valued at $12,850.[28] John Little still managed to continue to operate his cattle farm after his slaves were freed in 1862.

AN ESCAPED SLAVE AND A HOSPITAL:
THE CIVIL WAR COMES TO KALORAMA

With the arrival of thousands of Union troops in Washington in 1861, Hortense Prout, a twenty-year-old slave belonging to John Little, decided it provided an opportunity to make a run for her freedom. Little searched for her and found her in one of the Ohio camps, "completely rigged out in male attire." Hortense was turned over to Little and taken to jail.[29] Whether or not the Ohio company was aware that she was an escaped slave, or even that she was female, is uncertain. As a result of Hortense Prout's attempted escape to freedom, the site of John Little's farm in Kalorama Park is now included in the National Park Service's National Underground Railroad: Network to Freedom.

The Cliffbourne estate became the site of Cliffburne (a corruption of Cliffbourne), a United States Army cavalry barracks. The site provided an ideal location for cavalry horses, as it was already clear cut and used as farm and grazing land.

In 1862, following the Fifth U.S. Regiment's departure for the battlefield, the Cliffburne barracks were converted into the headquarters of the Invalid Corps under the direction of Lieutenant Colonel John Shaw Billings, a surgeon from Cincinnati. When Billings took charge of Cliffburne, he found the buildings and grounds "in an extremely filthy and dilapidated condition," with no drainage and no water within half a mile.[30] In order to be used as a hospital, additional buildings had to be added, along with 105 hospital tents, to accommodate up to one thousand patients.[31] Either the current tenant of the Cliffbourne estate or perhaps John Little had been raising and slaughtering cattle on the farm at the time, as "15 hundred loads of offal had to be cleared from the grounds and vicinity of the buildings."[32]

The hospital was one of the largest and one of the most comfortable in the District. Two wards of the hospital were devoted to Confederate soldiers who were brought in from Williamsburg. Caring for both Union and Confederate soldiers put the hospital in a delicate situation. The older residents of Georgetown and Washington, who were sympathetic to the South, brought food and drink to the hospital intended for the Confederate soldiers only. Family members of Congress and government officials also brought food, specifying that theirs should go only to the Union soldiers. Billings had to explain that the hospital could not accept gifts under such terms, and they were ultimately left for those who needed them most.[33]

Above: The Civil War hospital Cliffburne was located on the Cliffbourne estate. *Courtesy Library of Congress, Prints and Photographs Division.*

Left: Colonel John Shaw Billings, director of the Cliffburne Civil War Hospital. *Courtesy U.S. National Library of Medicine.*

While touring Cliffburne, William A. Bayley, a congressman from New York City, turned to Billings and asked, "You have got a lot of my boys here; I would like to do something for them, something that the papers will notice, you know. What do you think I had better give them?" Billings replied, "They have all got more or less scurvy, and I think fresh strawberries would do them

Poet Walt Whitman was a frequent visitor to the Cliffburne Civil War hospital. *Courtesy Library of Congress, Prints and Photographs Division.*

good. You might have a strawberry festival, and have a band here."[34] Bayley agreed, and the wounded were treated to strawberries and cream. The event was a great success.

In March 1863, Billings was transferred to field service and was assigned to the Fifth Corps of the Army of the Potomac. He was present at the bloody Battle of Gettysburg. In 1896, he was appointed director of the New York Public Library, a position he held until his death.

Poet Walt Whitman was a frequent visitor to the Cliffburne Hospital, spending many hours and entire nights sitting at the bedsides of soldiers. Whitman himself has often been described as a Civil War nurse, although his actual role was that of a very attentive visitor. In his poem "The Wound Dresser," Whitman wrote of his experiences in the Washington hospitals:

> *Thus in silence in dreams' projections,*
> *Returning, resuming, I thread my way through the hospitals;*
> *The hurt and wounded I pacify with soothing hand,*
> *I sit by the restless all the dark night—some are so young;*
> *Some suffer so much—I recall the experience sweet and sad.*

THE POSTBELLUM PERIOD

After the army relinquished Cliffbourne, Selah Reeve Hobbie's widow, Julianne, took up residence herself at Cliffbourne. It appears that she may have had to take up farming as well in order to support herself. In 1870, she purchased thirty-nine acres from Charles Francis Adams,[35] the son of John Quincy Adams, as an addition to the farmland she already owned. The small parcel ran along the northern boundary of the land and adjoined the Quaker cemetery. While not within the borders of Kalorama Triangle today, this additional tract of land became part of the Cliffbourne subdivision and is now the site of an apartment building at 1836 Adams Mill Road. Julianne Hobbie died in 1898 at the age of ninety-one.

By 1870, John Little was sixty-five years old and was still a farmer and living with his wife and three grown daughters. By now, Little only had three black employees on the estate and was also taking in boarders. John Little died in 1876 at the age of seventy-one and was buried at Congressional Cemetery. His estate, valued at over $1 million, was left to his five daughters. While not interested in continuing their father's farming and butcher business themselves, they quickly realized the value of the land they had just acquired.

By the 1880s, John Bassett Alley, a Massachusetts Republican elected to Congress from 1859 to 1867, had acquired the Cliffbourne estate. Alley may have had some connection with Selah Hobbie, as he had served as chairman of the Congressional Committee on the Post Office and Post Roads. Alley probably did not occupy Cliffbourne. In 1880, in what was basically a property swap, he sold it to General N.L. Jefferies for $20,000. In turn, Alley bought from Jefferies a sizeable mansion on McPherson Square at the corner of Fifteenth and K Streets for $30,000.

In 1890, Cliffbourne was the residence of Senator Lyman Rufus Casey of North Dakota, but an increase in his duties as senator made it necessary for him to move closer to the Capitol. The following year, it became home to inventor Marion C. Stone until his death in 1899, when it was torn down.

KALORAMA TRIANGLE JOINS THE DISTRICT

The District of Columbia Organic Act of 1871 revoked the Organic Act of 1801 and merged Washington City, Georgetown and Washington County into the single entity of the District of Columbia. Alexandria had seceded from the District in 1847. Strongly supported by Alexander Robey "Boss" Shepherd, this act also gave the District a democratically elected government consisting of a governor, a bicameral legislature and an elected non-voting delegate to the U.S. House of Representatives.

The act also provided for a Board of Public Works to make improvements to the city. President Ulysses S. Grant appointed Shepherd, the board's most influential member, as the city's second governor in 1873. As governor, Shepherd embarked on a citywide revitalization plan that included paving streets and installing a sewer system. However, charges in 1874 that the D.C. government was corrupt and nearing bankruptcy led Congress to abolish the office of governor in favor of direct rule. Congress created a temporary three-man commission to run the District, and the position of the non-voting delegate was abolished. The commission became permanent in 1874, with Congress serving as the District legislature. The local government was made permanent by the Organic Act of 1878. Until 1967, three presidentially appointed District commissioners would run the city.

Shepherd remained in Washington until 1876, when he declared personal bankruptcy and moved with his family to Batopilas, Mexico. In Mexico, he was able to rebuild his fortune in the silver mining business and instituted many of the same reforms he had implemented while governor in the District of Columbia. Shepherd only made two return trips to Washington. He died in Batopilas in 1902 from complications following appendix surgery. His body was returned to Washington and buried in a large vault in Rock Creek Cemetery. After his death, his widow moved to a house at 1917 Kalorama Road.

CROSSING ROCK CREEK

Three Bridges and a Railroad

In the short span of one year, between 1887 and 1888, three large public transportation projects were undertaken—replacing the wooden Woodley Lane Bridge over Rock Creek Park, creating the Rock Creek Railway and extending Connecticut Avenue to the north above Florida Avenue. These projects were manipulated by congressmen and real estate developers whose main interests were to protect their investments in Washington Heights and the future suburb of Chevy Chase. As a result of these projects, development in Washington Heights exploded in the 1890s.

WOODLEY LANE BRIDGE

Until the 1890s, crossing Rock Creek north of Florida Avenue was a challenge. The only means to cross the creek was to travel up Columbia Road, onto Woodley Lane (now the 2300 block of Nineteenth Street and Belmont Road) and then over a wooden bridge at the foot of the street. A bridge had stood on the site at the time of the Civil War, but it washed away in 1875, as did its replacement in 1889.

The deep valley in which Rock Creek sits created two steep grades on either side of the bridge, which were very difficult to ascend and descend and were considered dangerous. Farmers on their way to market would avoid the bridge, traveling by way of Georgetown, as it was impossible for horse teams to haul a load of produce up or down the steep grades. But at the same time, the road was the city's closest outlet to the northwest. The next was at Klingle Ford four miles away.

In January 1888, the Senate began discussion of a bill to construct a new bridge to replace the old Woodley Lane Bridge. Senator George Graham Vest of Missouri presented a petition signed by various residents and property holders along Woodley Lane asking for the speedy passage of the bill. There was very little time allotted for discussion. By the end of February 1888, Congress authorized the construction of the bridge. The Citizens' Committee of One Hundred had objected to funding the bridge on the basis that if any money was to be spent, it should go to the eastern part of the city. There was also concern expressed by some members of Congress that this bridge would only benefit land speculators and property owners. In fact, when the Groton Iron Tanks Company, contracted to build the bridge, realized the $35,000 appropriated for the project was not enough, Washington Heights developer George Truesdell, Woodley Park developer John Floyd Waggaman and several others contributed $5,000 each in order that construction on the bridge could continue. Construction was completed in 1890.

Within ten years, the bridge was considered dangerous and inadequate to serve traffic to the northwest suburbs. The only remains of the bridge today are a single thirty- by thirty-foot portion of one of the abutments and two small stone piers that once held up the bridge's trusses.

ROCK CREEK RAILWAY

The same month that Congress authorized the new Woodley Lane Bridge in 1888, it began discussion of a bill to create the District's second electric streetcar railroad, the Rock Creek Railway. By now, many were realizing that, like the Woodley Lane Bridge, a railway through Washington Heights was another special interest project on the part of some congressmen and land developers. Representative David Bremner Henderson from Iowa wanted to amend the bill's title to call it a "bill to boom real estate in the District of Columbia." He declared that the Woodley Lane and Rock Creek areas were regions where "nabobs" (persons of conspicuous wealth or high status) were going to flourish in the future, and he did not want to "encourage their growth by legislation." Henderson later realized that the Woodley Lane Bridge and Rock Creek Railway bills were timed so that the grading for the bridge would be done at the District's expense and the new railway company would have the benefit of both the grading and the bridge without paying for either.[36]

The Rock Creek Railway was chartered on June 23, 1888, by developer Francis Griffith Newlands. The charter was for a single track, to be powered either by horse, cable or electricity, running from the intersection of Connecticut Avenue and Boundary Street (now Florida Avenue) up Columbia Road to Woodley Lane and connecting to Woodley Park.

Congressman Henderson's concerns about nabobs were not unwarranted—they were already there. The congressionally appointed board of directors of the Rock Creek Railway Company included wealthy Kalorama Triangle residents and developers, such as George Truesdell as its president, Samuel W. Woodward, Otis F. Presbrey, Lawrence Sands, Samuel S. Shedd and Robert J. Fisher. The company also had powerful and vested congressional supporters, including Senator William M. Stewart, who was a partner in Newlands's venture, the Chevy Chase Land Company.

The Rock Creek Railway began limited service on Florida Avenue between Connecticut Avenue NW and Eighteenth Street NW in 1890. The same year, Newlands, along with Senator Stewart and Lieutenant Colonel George Augustus Ames, launched the Chevy Chase Land Company venture to develop a residential streetcar suburb for Washington, D.C. Newlands and his partners had been in the process of buying up undeveloped land north of Rock Creek in northwestern Washington, D.C., and southern Montgomery County, Maryland, since the late 1880s. In what might be the subject of antitrust laws today, many of the officers and principal stockholders of the Chevy Chase Land Company served on the board of the Rock Creek Railway Company as well.[37]

Francis Griffith Newlands. *Courtesy Library of Congress, Prints and Photographs Division.*

The trestle streetcar bridge over Rock Creek Park between Calvert Street and Connecticut Avenue, circa 1891. *HAER. Courtesy Library of Congress, Prints and Photographs Division.*

Streetcar access from the city would be necessary to ensure Chevy Chase's place as a viable Washington suburb. But the usefulness of the Woodley Lane Bridge for this purpose was questionable. It had not been designed to accommodate streetcars well, with its circuitous route across the park and steep grades. In 1890, only one year after the completion of the Woodley Lane Bridge, the Rock Creek Railway proposed a new route to the District commissioners. This route would bypass the Woodley Lane Bridge and cross Rock Creek on yet another bridge. This bridge—which the Rock Creek Railway would construct at its own cost—would be seventy-five feet higher than the Woodley Lane Bridge. The route would run through the Cliffbourne estate, which Newlands had his eye on and would purchase three years later, pass over the new bridge and connect to Connecticut Avenue toward Chevy Chase. Congress quickly moved to re-charter the company to incorporate the new route. The bridge was completed in 1891, and the following year, the Rock Creek Railway line was extended up Eighteenth Street and across the bridge.

The railway line was completed in 1893, financed by the Chevy Chase Land Company. But its construction was not without problems. D.C. laws prevented electric railways from using overhead electrical wires within the original federal city, but this did not apply to areas north of Florida Avenue. Senator Hale proposed a bill opposing the use of overhead wires for the railway. But Senator William Stewart, an obvious champion of the interests of the company, protested the bill, as it would mandate the laying of cable, the cost of which would have to be borne by the company at the expense of laying roads.[38] The bill was defeated.

In 1895, Congress authorized the purchase of the Washington and Georgetown Railway Company by the Rock Creek Railway, forming the Capital Traction Company, with George Truesdell serving again as president. This marked the end of the Rock Creek Railway as a unique entity. In 1899, as one of his earliest commissions, Kalorama resident and noted architect Waddy Wood would design the Capitol Traction waiting station and streetcar turnaround (the "loop") at the foot of Calvert Street before the bridge.

EXTENDING CONNECTICUT AVENUE

In 1887, the District commissioners began proceedings to extend Connecticut Avenue to Woodley Lane and widen Columbia Road to better accommodate the vehicle-using public traffic leaving the city to the north. The first plan for extending Connecticut Avenue through Kalorama was to cut a direct path from Florida Avenue to the Woodley Lane Bridge.

In 1888, the commissioners began land condemnation proceedings to extend Connecticut Avenue above Florida Avenue. Hoping to influence the course of the avenue, the year before, George Truesdell had brought his subdivision, Truesdell's Addition to Washington Heights, on the market with an optimistically named one-block street, Connecticut Avenue Extended (now Ashmead Place). Initially, it appeared that Truesdell's plan had paid off. The extension was to be run to Truesdell's Connecticut Avenue Extended and connect to the Woodley Lane Bridge.

Washington Heights property owners met with the District commissioners protesting against the planned approaches to the bridge. This route would have meant certain condemnation of properties along the route. Samuel Woodward protested against the lowering of the grade on Wyoming Avenue, as it would damage his property. Thomas J.D. Fuller, living at the top of Ashmead Place, contended that the grading of the streets and running Connecticut Avenue to Woodley Lane via Ashmead Place would cause damage to his property. Meeting with

Francis Newlands's northern extension of Connecticut Avenue put pressure on the District commissioners to complete its southern extension above Florida Avenue. This is a view looking south from Woodley Park with the avenue abruptly ending at Rock Creek. *Courtesy Library of Congress, Prints and Photographs Division.*

continuous protests, lawsuits and lack of funding, the commissioners finally halted the project.

Between 1894 and 1895, the city's District engineer commissioner was at work on an amended Permanent System of Highways Act of 1893, which would still require streets in the subdivisions outside Washington City to adhere as closely as possible to the L'Enfant plan. Special attention was given to the location of Connecticut Avenue Extended. Resulting grades, existing public and private improvements, the Rock Creek crossing and public convenience were all taken into consideration in the eventual compromise route. It would use the lower few blocks of Columbia Road, continue through a widened Connecticut Avenue Extended, bypass Truesdell's block and cross the valley. This solution missed the existing homes of the affluent residents along the way.

By 1891, the Chevy Chase Land Company was busy at work on the northern extension of Connecticut Avenue, from Rock Creek to its new suburb. The company had constructed a straight line from Chevy Chase to the edge of Rock Creek. Senator Stewart was not pleased with the District's proposed circuitous approach from the south and did not see how it would connect. Stewart amended the appropriations bill for Connecticut Avenue to require a straight connection to his section of Connecticut Avenue. Senator James McMillan worked out a compromise that created a circular reservation on the south side of the future Connecticut Avenue Bridge, which would serve to connect the two misaligned sections of Connecticut Avenue.

Francis Newlands later served as a Democratic representative from Nevada between 1893 and 1903. Newlands became a senator from Nevada in 1903 and served until his death in 1917. He was a also member of the

Senate subcommittee that investigated the 1912 sinking of RMS *Titanic*. A self-avowed racist, he made an unsuccessful bid for president in 1912 on a platform that called for a constitutional amendment to repeal African Americans' right to vote.

CONNECTICUT AVENUE (TAFT MEMORIAL) BRIDGE

The construction of a bridge to replace the Woodley Lane Bridge and connect Connecticut Avenue Extended to Newland's completed part of Connecticut Avenue was not proposed until 1897. In March of that year, Congress authorized an appropriation and a competition for the design of the bridge. The winning design was submitted by George S. Morison, a graduate of Harvard Law School and a well-known railroad bridge engineer. With some modifications to Morison's design, Congress appropriated $250,000 to begin the bridge's construction. The superstructure was finished by the District Construction Company in 1907. The eagle lampposts along its side were designed by Ernest Bairstow, who later carved the sculptured features of the Lincoln Memorial. The iconic pair of cast-concrete lions on either side of the bridge was designed by Roland Hinton Perry.

When it was completed in 1907, it was the largest concrete bridge in the world. Due to its extended period of construction, continuous lack of

The Connecticut Avenue Bridge under construction in 1905. The old Woodley Lane Bridge was left in place during construction to avoid any interruption in traffic. *Courtesy of the Washingtoniana Room, Martin Luther King Library.*

The Connecticut Avenue Bridge soon after it opened to traffic in 1907. *Courtesy Library of Congress, Prints and Photographs Division.*

appropriations and skyrocketing expenses, the bridge was nicknamed the Million Dollar Bridge. In 1931, the bridge was rededicated as the William H. Taft Memorial Bridge, as former president Taft had lived nearby at 2215 Wyoming Avenue and liked to take walks over it. The bridge was added to the National Register of Historic Places in 2003.

The extension of Connecticut Avenue above Florida Avenue divided Washington Heights into two separate and distinct neighborhoods. The neighborhood west of Connecticut Avenue, now known as Sheridan-Kalorama, would develop later than Kalorama Triangle, with large lots and grand, individually commissioned, freestanding houses that became the residences of Washington's elite. To the east of Connecticut Avenue, Kalorama Triangle would become a solidly middle- and upper-middle-class neighborhood with a mix of large, single homes, rows of town houses and apartment buildings.

This division remains today. Recently, during an open house for a condominium on the west side of Connecticut Avenue, the realtor was asked by a prospective buyer about the neighborhood. The realtor replied, "Don't worry, people usually stick to their own side of Connecticut Avenue."

CALVERT STREET (DUKE ELLINGTON MEMORIAL) BRIDGE

By 1911, the Calvert Street trestle bridge was failing. In an effort to reinforce it and extend its life, the overhang was reduced and the road narrowed to twenty-six feet. It was so narrow that streetcars and the growing number of automobiles had to share the same surface. The towers were reinforced with timber cribbing. But by 1917, it was clear that the trestle bridge needed to be replaced.

The District commissioners commissioned local architect George Oakley Totten Jr. to design the new bridge. Totten was an École des Beaux-Arts–trained and prominent local architect who designed many private mansions, including the Edward Hamlin Everett house at 1606 Twenty-third Street NW (now the residence of the Turkish ambassador) and the Christian Hauge House at 2349 Massachusetts Avenue NW (now the Cameroonian Chancellery). Over a number of years, Totten submitted numerous plans to the District commissioners and the Commission of Fine Arts. Various designs of the bridge were rejected as they were too costly, had too many arches or were too monumental and elaborate and would overshadow the prized Connecticut Avenue Bridge.

Ten years after Totten was asked to submit a design for the new bridge, nothing had been done but to continue patching the old bridge, whose collapse was predicted by March 1934. Finally, in 1933, the Commission of Fine Arts approved the design of a masonry bridge with three arches by French architect Paul Phillipe Cret and the firm of Modjeski, Masters & Chase. Cret was born in Lyon, France, and, like Totten, had been educated at the École des Beaux-Arts in Paris. Modjeski was born in Poland and attended the École des Beaux-Arts as well. He began his career working with George Morrison, who had designed the Connecticut Avenue Bridge, and became the chief engineer for construction of the Calvert Street Bridge.

The original trestle bridge was moved downstream on rollers to make way for the construction of the new bridge. It was pulled by four winches, with one horse to a winch, and was moved eighty feet in seven hours and fifteen minutes. It was used as a detour until the new bridge was opened to traffic in 1935 and was then demolished. The Calvert Street Bridge was rededicated as the Duke Ellington Memorial Bridge following the death of the Washington native and famous bandleader in 1974 and is a D.C. historic landmark.

In 1985, District officials devised a plan to erect eight-foot fences along both the Taft Bridge and the Calvert Street Bridge to prevent suicides, which

Aerial view of the Calvert Street Bridge. *HAER. Courtesy Library of Congress, Prints and Photographs Division.*

were numbering an average of five per year. Although Congress approved the new high fences for both bridges, there was much contention about the aesthetic effect on the Taft Bridge, and as a result, only the fences on the Calvert Street Bridge were installed.

FROM COUNTRY ESTATES TO SUBURBIA

Developing Kalorama Triangle

After the Civil War, the city of Washington began to grow beyond its original limits. But until 1872, the land in Kalorama Triangle still had only three owners: the Corcorans, John Little and Julianne Hobbie. Starting in the early 1870s, property owners in Washington County began subdividing their large tracts of land into building lots and streets and then recording them with the office of the city surveyor.

The Corcorans and John Little's daughters were the first landowners in Kalorama Triangle to begin dividing up their properties in the 1870s. As the first, the Corcorans' subdivision, Washington Heights, became the de facto name by which the land falling north of Florida Avenue, between Connecticut Avenue and Eighteenth Street, encompassing what is now Kalorama Triangle, would be referred to for years to follow.

By 1889, Washington Heights already had seven new subdivisions, and real estate agents began promoting the area for the more affluent buyers. An 1891 advertisement in the *Washington Post* by the firm Fitch, Fox, and Brown read:

> *Washington Heights is nearly 200 feet above the river, and from this property commanding and picturesque views are had in every direction, especially up the magnificent Rock Creek Valley. Immediately adjoining are the finest suburban residences in the District. The streets are paved,*

sidewalks are laid, water, gas, and sewerage—combines all of the comforts of the city with the delights of the country; scarcely ten minutes' drive from the city hall renders this property most desirable for either winter or summer residences.[39]

Still, at this time, few were interested in purchasing real estate in Washington Heights. The Permanent System of Highway Act of 1893, along with a financial panic that same year, had a major dampening effect on real estate sales in Washington Heights' subdivisions. The act called for the development of street plans that would be compatible and consistent with the original L'Enfant plan. It remained unclear for five years afterward if the uncoordinated development of the various subdivisions throughout the newly consolidated Washington would have to be reconfigured to conform to the plan. However, by 1892, nine out of ten of Kalorama's subdivisions had already been created. A few started buying lots along well-established routes—Columbia Road, Kalorama Road and Wyoming Avenue—streets less likely to be affected by the implementation of the Highway Act and the northern extension of the numbered streets.

But beyond these few pioneer homeowners, lots in the newly created subdivisions were not selling. No one wanted to invest in a house lot, build a house and later have it condemned to create a new street in order to extend L'Enfant's plan through Washington Heights. Even the extension of the Metropolitan streetcar line up Columbia Road in 1896 did not result in an immediate rise in lot purchases. A *Washington Post* article stated that at that time, Washington Heights consisted of a few spasmodic dwellings along Columbia Road, notably Cliffbourne, the Little property and the residence of F.P.B. Sands.[40] Finally, in 1898, an amended Highway Act was passed that grandfathered the subdivisions that had been established prior to 1893. Then the building boom finally began.

KALORAMA TRIANGLE'S ORIGINAL SUBDIVISIONS

Corcoran's Washington Heights

The first landowners to subdivide their holdings in Kalorama Triangle were William M. and William Wilson "W.W." Corcoran. W.W. Corcoran was the son of Thomas Corcoran, an Irish immigrant and a four-time mayor of Georgetown. W.W. Corcoran would start working in the dry goods business and build one of the century's great family dynasties.

In 1828, William Corcoran took control of a large amount of real estate from his father, including a large section of Kalorama and Kalorama Triangle. The Corcorans continued to buy land throughout the city into the 1860s, and in 1872, they put their land north of Florida Avenue on the market as Washington Heights. At this time, Washington Heights was not easily accessible. The first horse-drawn streetcar that served the southern edge of the neighborhood, the Connecticut Avenue and Park Railway, provided service up Connecticut Avenue to Boundary Street (Florida Avenue), where it stopped. The grade was too steep for the horse-drawn streetcars and was a challenge for other horse-drawn vehicles as well. Yet a few individuals saw the advantage of the breezy hilltop, and the panoramic vista outweighed the costs of the trek up the hill.

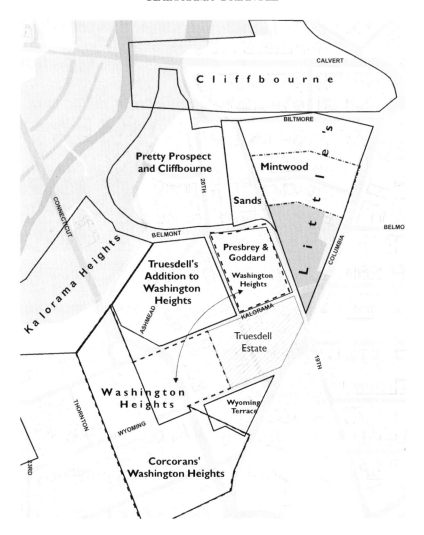

The original subdivisions of Kalorama Triangle. *Map by Matthew B. Gilmore.*

Dr. William Tindall

The first house built in Corcoran's subdivision, on the southernmost point of Washington Heights, was the home of Dr. William Tindall. Following service in the Union army during the Civil War, Tindall moved to Washington, D.C., to study medicine at Georgetown University. He then served sixty-three years with the District of Columbia government and was a longtime secretary to the District commissioners. Tindall was also a prominent local historian, writing often for the *Records of the Columbia Historical Society.*

Dr. William Tindall. *Courtesy Library of Congress, Prints and Photographs Division.*

On the back of a photograph of the house, William Tindall wrote a nostalgic personal note about his years there: "It is doubtful that a more harmonious family group could be found than that of the one girl and three boys who filled that home with glee and good fellowship, from the spring of 1881 until the summer of 1907, under the supervision of a mother who 'understood.' The world owes me nothing on the score of domestic felicity."

In 1907, Dr. Tindall's house was razed to make way for construction of a mansion for Alvin Mason Lothrop; today, this is home to the Trade Representative of the Russian Federation.

The second house built in Washington Heights stood behind Dr. Tindall's house at 2010 Columbia Road. It was built in 1892 by architect William M. Poindexter for Miss E.F. Free. The house was the first of a tradition of embassies and diplomats choosing Kalorama Triangle for their homes. In 1900, the Brazilian minister, J.F. de Assis-Brasil, moved into the house, and it became the Brazilian legation. It was razed sometime after 1943 and is now the site of the parking lot for the Trade Representative of the Russian Federation at 2001 Connecticut Avenue.

Architect William Poindexter moved to Washington after the Civil War and worked at the office of the supervising architect of the government. After a few years of office work, Poindexter went into business for himself. He also served on the faculty of the Corcoran School of Science and Arts and Columbia University, now The George Washington University.

Above: The Tindall house once stood at 2001 Connecticut Avenue. *Courtesy Library of Congress, Prints and Photographs Division.*

Below: This house once stood at 2010 Columbia Road and became the Brazilian legation in 1900. Photo circa 1920–21. *Courtesy Library of Congress, Prints and Photographs Division.*

Presbrey and Goddard's Subdivision

In 1882, Dr. Otis F. Fletcher Presbrey, who had been appointed a tax assessor for the state of New York by Abraham Lincoln, and Elisha Goddard, a clerk at the Treasury Department, combined and subdivided their holdings in Washington Heights to create Presbrey and Goddard's subdivision. Their landholdings were in two noncontiguous sections. The southwest section reached west over Connecticut Avenue, partway up the 2000 block of Kalorama Road. The second part was an isolated square block in the center of Washington Heights between Nineteenth and Twentieth Streets and Kalorama and Belmont Road. After the construction of Tindall's house in Corcoran's Washington Heights, Presbrey and Goddard's subdivision was the next to see any development.

Samuel Walter Woodward (2015 Wyoming Avenue)

The first house in Presbrey and Goddard's subdivision at 2015 Wyoming Avenue was built in 1886 for Samuel Walter Woodward and was designed by architect Eugene Clarence Gardner. Woodward selected the location of the highest elevation in Kalorama Triangle, sitting at the top of the rise of the hill on Connecticut Avenue before descending into the Rock Creek Valley.

Samuel Woodward was born in Damariscotta, Maine, on December 13, 1848. In 1873, he established a dry goods business in Chelsea, Massachusetts, with partner Alvin Lothrop. After opening several stores in the Boston area, they joined with Charles E. Cochrane and moved to Washington in 1880. Woodward and Lothrop would not only be business partners but would also become neighbors when Lothrop built his stately mansion just south of Woodward's on the site of the Tindall house.

Woodward, Lothrop & Cochrane opened its first store in Washington at 705 Market Space at the intersection of Pennsylvania Avenue and Seventh Street NW (now the site of the United States Navy Memorial). Woodward and Lothrop bought out Cochrane's share of the partnership, and the new store was renamed Woodward & Lothrop. In 1886, it moved to its ultimate location at the corner of Eleventh and F Streets NW. By 1897, after several expansions, the store occupied almost the entire block surrounded by Tenth, Eleventh, F and G Streets NW. In 1898 and 1902, the buildings were renovated behind a new façade facing G Street designed by noted Chicago architect Henry Ives Cobb, who would later design several town houses on

Left: Samuel Walter Woodward. *In Merrill, Men of Mark.*

Below: Samuel Woodward built his impressive mansion at 2015 Wyoming Avenue in 1886. *Courtesy the Historical Society of Washington, D.C.*

the 2000 block of Columbia Road. The building remained the flagship store of Woodward & Lothrop until it closed in 1994.

When architect Eugene Clarence Gardner moved to Washington, D.C. from Springfield, Massachusetts, in 1886, he found himself in charge of several large commissions, including the Woodward house and a neighboring house at 2011 Wyoming Avenue. Gardner was also a writer and wrote several architectural books, most notably a fictional work entitled *The House that Jill Built: After Jack's Had Proved a Failure*. In this book on home architecture, Gardner seems to express his own experiences in working with married couples in designing and building houses. The story involves a bride-to-be who demands a better home than the one her fiancé promises to build. Throughout the book, she establishes herself as an expert on domestic architecture.

In addition to merchandizing, Woodward turned much of his attention to civic services. In addition to being president of the Young Men's Christian Association, he also served as the chairman of the committee of the Washington Sanitary Housing Company, which was composed of prominent citizens who sought better housing conditions in the District. Kalorama neighbor and real estate developer George Truesdell served as the vice-chairman of the committee. Woodward assigned each committee member a neglected district to make monthly, personal inspections and report back to the committee. Woodward, along with George Truesdell, ex-senator John B. Henderson and others, was assigned the "second division," which consisted of Rock Creek to Fifteenth Street NW.

Samuel Woodward died in 1917. His house was razed in 1926 for the construction of 2101 Connecticut Avenue.

Eliza Barker House (2011 Wyoming Avenue)

A large Queen Anne–style house that once stood just next to Samuel Woodward's mansion at 2011 Wyoming Avenue was built on speculation in 1886 by George Truesdell and was designed by Woodward's architect, Eugene Clarence Gardner, as well. Prominent local builder and architect Robert I. Fleming was contracted to build a two-story brick garage with sleeping quarters in the rear of the house in 1895.

Although of wood construction, this Queen Anne–style house was by no means modest and echoed some of the opulence of its large brick neighbor, the Woodward mansion. The first floor had a reception hall, a parlor, two libraries, a dining room, a pantry, a kitchen and an enclosed porch from the

The Eliza Barker house once stood next to Samuel Woodward's house at 2011 Wyoming Avenue. It is now the location of the parking lot for 2101 Connecticut Avenue. The home of Charles H. Heyl at 2009 Wyoming stands to the right. *Courtesy Library of Congress, Prints and Photographs Division.*

library, in addition to the large front porch. The second floor consisted of a living room, five bedrooms, two baths, a lavatory and three porches. The third floor housed three bedrooms, two baths and a large storeroom. The basement had a bedroom with hot and cold running water, a billiard room, a laundry, a wood room and a bathroom.

The house was first purchased by Mrs. Eliza Barker. Eliza Barker may have started a mini-competition with her neighbor Samuel Woodward with the design of her carriage house by prominent local architect Robert I. Fleming. Woodward followed suit and had his carriage house designed in 1902 by noted Chicago architect Henry Isaac Cobb, who also designed the new façade for the Woodward & Lothrop store on F Street the same year.

Eliza Barker left the house to her daughter Flora. In 1918, Flora leased the house to the Serbian ambassador, but the following year, the house was put on the market in order to settle the estate. In 1921, it was home to Representative Wallace H. White of Maine. The house, like many others in Kalorama Triangle, fell on hard times during the Depression. In 1935, it was home to Mrs. Mildred C. Fleming, who had turned it into a guesthouse, and after the Second World War, it was converted to apartments. It was demolished in 1954 to make way for the two-level parking garage behind 2101 Connecticut Avenue.

Mrs. Alexander Robey Shepherd (1917 Kalorama Road)

In 1887, Eugene Gardner designed a similar house to Eliza's Barker's house across the street from George Truesdell's summer estate Mangasset at 1917 Kalorama Road. Its builder, J.H. Lane, was also the builder of former Missouri senator John B. Henderson's mansion on Sixteenth Street, known as Mrs. Henderson's Castle. A 1920 *Washington Post* photo caption announcing the sale of the house stated that the mansion was erected by former governor Alexander Shepherd and had been occupied by his widow since his death.[41]

In 1901, former Michigan congressman Henry W. Seymour and his wife bought the house, and Mrs. Shepherd continued to live there until it was sold

The house that once stood at 1917 Kalorama Road was the home of former District governor Alexander Shepherd's widow. *Courtesy Library of Congress, Prints and Photographs Division.*

in 1920 to Mrs. Joseph P. Tumulty. She was the wife of President Wilson's personal secretary, Joseph Tumulty, who remained with Wilson through his entire administration. This proved difficult at times, as the second Mrs. Wilson asked her husband that Tumulty be fired, but to no avail. Tumulty remained in the house for only eight years. He became a successful lawyer and, in 1928, bought a newly constructed house at 16 Kalorama Circle. The house at 1917 Kalorama was razed to make way for the five-story apartment building now on the site.

Robert Jones Fisher (1915 Kalorama Road)

Tumulty's immediate neighbor to his right at 1915 Kalorama Road was Robert Strettell Jones Fisher, whose house was built around the same time as Shepherd's. Fisher was born in York, Pennsylvania, of Quaker descent and was a graduate of Pennsylvania College and the Albany Law School. He began work for the U.S. Patent Office in 1876 as a third assistant examiner and gradually worked his way through the ranks of the examining corps, including the Appeal Board of Examiners-in-Chief, becoming assistant commissioner of patents in 1889.

In 1891, at the age of forty-three, he resigned as assistant commissioner of patents to accept an appointment as general counsel of the Eastern Railroad Association. Fisher had already demonstrated his interests in railways. In 1888, when the Rock Creek Railway was incorporated, Fisher was one of the many Kalorama Triangle residents who became a charter member of the board. Fisher died at his home on Kalorama Road in 1932 and is buried in Rock Creek Cemetery. The former house is now the site of the Connecticut Gardens Apartment building that was built in 1939.

Row Houses in Presbrey and Goddard's Subdivision

The first row houses to be built in Presbrey and Goddard's subdivision were built in 1899 at 1901–5 Kalorama Road and 2308–12 Nineteenth Street by prominent Kalorama builder John H. Nolan. They were designed by architect George S. Cooper, who was one of the first architects specializing in the town houses in Kalorama Triangle, having built the neighborhood's first town houses on Wyoming Avenue in 1895. Unlike the town houses Cooper had also designed on the 2000 block of Columbia Road in 1899, this set of houses was done in the then somewhat passé Romanesque Revival style.

The Romanesque Revival style was prominent in American cities from 1880 to 1900 and was popularized by architect Henry Hobson Richardson and his followers. One of the most prominent features of the Romanesque Revival style was the use of semicircular arches over doorways and windows supported with square or round columns. Romanesque Revival houses often had asymmetrical proportions, employing rounded or square bays and dark materials, to create an impression of massiveness and weight. Rough-cut or rusticated stone was commonly used for the basement level, above windows and doors and between floors.

Farther north along Nineteenth Street at numbers 2318–34 and around the corner at 1908–14 Belmont Road are two groups of Georgian, terrace-style town houses, popular in the British Isles during the eighteenth century. They were built in 1910 by the team of architect Albert H. Beers and builder Harry Wardman and are sometimes referred to as Kalorama's Wardman Row.

Harry Wardman was a prodigious real estate developer in Washington, D.C., during the early twentieth century. His buildings included town houses, middle-class apartment buildings, freestanding houses, landmark hotels and luxury apartment buildings. He began his career by building affordable apartments and simple private dwellings throughout the city that provided affordable and family-friendly accommodations for federal

Kalorama Triangle's Wardman Row on Nineteenth Street. *Photo by the author.*

Developer Harry Wardman. *Courtesy Library of Congress, Prints and Photographs Division.*

employees and their families. He partnered with architect Albert H. Beers, who served as his in-house architect for many of his projects. Like Wardman, Beers began by designing affordable apartments for federal employees and their families. Beers is credited with designing more apartments in a six-year period than any other Washington architect, ranging from small two- and three-story buildings to large, luxurious apartment buildings.

After Wardman teamed with Beers, they moved on to building larger, single-family houses and more luxurious apartment buildings, which included the Dresden at 2126 Connecticut Avenue NW (1909) and the Chastleton on Sixteenth Street. Wardman and Beers were also responsible for much of the original development along the west side of the 1800 block of Columbia Road. Ultimately, these buildings were replaced with one-story storefront buildings when the block was zoned for commercial use in 1929.

After the death of Albert Beers in 1911, Wardman moved to building luxury hotels, such as the Wardman Park Hotel (1916), now the site of the Marriott Wardman Park Hotel, and the Hay-Adams Hotel, designed by Turkish architect Mihran Mesrobian. Another Wardman landmark of this period is the British Embassy. By the late 1920s, Wardman had become a very wealthy man, but he lost most of his $30 million fortune in the stock market crash of 1929, although he continued to build middle-class homes until his death in 1938.

WYOMING TERRACE (FLAGG'S SUBDIVISION)

In 1888, the District commissioners widened Columbia Road, then one of the most important roads leading from the city, between Florida Avenue and Nineteenth Street, from thirty-three to sixty-five feet in width. The following year, Edmund H. Flagg brought his subdivision, Wyoming Terrace, onto the market. But even with an improved Columbia Road, these lots sat idly until they slowly began to sell in 1895.

The first town houses in Kalorama Triangle were built in 1895 and were located at 2012–14 Wyoming Avenue, along with a detached house at 2010 Wyoming, all now the site of the Wyoming Plaza condominium building. These three houses were designed by George S. Cooper for the real estate firm of Davidson & Davidson. Like many real estate firms at the time, Davidson & Davidson began as real estate developers, acting as financial intermediaries between contractors, architects and clients. Davidson & Davidson had an early and long history in Kalorama Triangle. In the 1880s, the firm brokered the sale of fifteen acres in Kalorama to George Truesdell; this became the site of his estate Managasset and his 1887 subdivision, Truesdell's Addition to Washington Heights.

The development of the 2000 block of Columbia Road in Wyoming Terrace was due mostly to the efforts of real estate developer Arthur Coswill, who produced a mix of Gothic- and Romanesque-style,

Houses on the 2000 block of Columbia Road. *Photo by the author.*

freestanding houses and duplex town houses along the western side of the street in the 1890s. Until the construction of the Wyoming apartments in 1909 at 2022 Columbia Road, this location, if only briefly, afforded a magnificent panorama of the city.

In 1898, Coswill constructed a pair of Gothic Revival–style duplex town houses at 2003–5 Columbia Road. They were designed by prominent Chicago architect Henry Ives Cobb, who had come to Washington in 1898 to produce a plan for American University. In Chicago, Cobb had received a significant number of commissions for important public buildings, major residences and commercial buildings, plus the Fisheries Building, one of the ten principal buildings at the World's Columbian Exposition in 1893. His largest commission was the Chicago post office and federal building, completed in 1905.

One of the unique features of these Columbia Road town houses was the use of oriel (bay) windows spanning the second and third stories. The interior plan placed the entertaining spaces on the second floor, known as the *piano nobile*. The ground floor was reserved for a reception room, a stair hall and service areas, including a kitchen.

In 1899, George Cooper joined with builder John Sherman and followed suit with three Romanesque-style town houses: a duplex pair at 2015–13 Columbia Road and a third, taller building at 2011 Columbia Road

That same year, Arthur Coswill built two freestanding Romanesque-style houses on the block, one with architect William Conley at 2009

Columbia and the other with Henry Ives Cobb at 2001 Columbia. Not long after it was built, George Young, second secretary of the British Embassy, took up residence at 2009 Columbia Road, becoming the second diplomat to reside in Kalorama Triangle. It later became the home of the Greek Legation and the Italian World War Veterans Association and is now an art gallery.

The freestanding, red brick Romanesque Revival–style house at 2007 Columbia Road was also built by Arthur Coswill and designed by Appleton P. Clark for socialite Christina Somerville. It was the only house on the block that was not built on speculation. Appleton Clark would later work with Christian Heurich on plans to build a large apartment building on the site of Kalorama Park and would design the Sterling apartment building on 1915 Calvert Street and Thomas A. Dobyns's house on 1957 Biltmore Street.

Christina Somerville was the daughter of plumbing supply magnate Thomas Somerville. After her father died and Christina received her inheritance, she chose to build a new home in Flagg's subdivision. Christina ended up suing her brothers, as she thought that she was not getting her share of her inheritance from her father's estate. At some point, Christina became Mrs. Christina Somerville, having married naval Captain William M. Somerville. She later moved to the Kenesaw Apartments at Sixteenth and Irving Streets, where she died in 1938.

The Wood-Deming Houses (2017–19 Connecticut Avenue)

The two town houses at 2017–19 Connecticut Avenue were designed and built by prominent local architect Waddy Butler Wood in 1903. Wood was a prominent American architect of the early twentieth century and was also a resident of Kalorama Triangle. His first commissions were two streetcar barns—the Metropolitan Railroad's East Capitol Street Car Barn and the Georgetown Car Barn, then known as Union Station, for the Capital Traction Company—as well as the company's streetcar loop waiting station on Calvert Street.

During this time, Wood turned his attention to residential architecture and designed several homes in Kalorama Triangle. He designed a Georgian Revival–style house for Arthur Keith at 2210 Twentieth Street in 1898. That same year, Wood turned to the Arts and Crafts style for the house at 1850 Mintwood Place and for four houses at the intersection of Cliffbourne Place and Calvert Streets in 1900 and 1901.

Wood-Deming houses at 2017–19 Connecticut Avenue. *HABS. Courtesy Library of Congress, Prints and Photographs Division.*

Wood, along with Edward Donn Jr. and William I. Deming, formed the firm of Wood, Donn and Deming in 1902. The following year, Wood designed the pair of houses at 2017–19 Connecticut Avenue, one to be occupied by himself and the other by his new partner Deming. Number 2017 Connecticut Avenue is now the Embassy of Malta.

The firm of Wood, Donn and Deming was highly successful in Washington, D.C. One of the firm's most notable buildings was the 1907 Masonic Temple located at the intersection of Thirteenth Street, H Street and New York Avenue NW, which is now the National Museum of Women

Architect Waddy Butler Wood.
Courtesy Library of Congress, Prints and Photographs Division.

in the Arts. Despite the successes of Wood, Donn and Deming, the firm was dissolved in 1912, and Wood went back into practice by himself. He did not design any additional houses in Kalorama Triangle after this point.

Benjamin Bradford House (2034 Wyoming Avenue)

The house that stands at 2034 Wyoming Avenue was designed and built by real estate broker Benjamin B. Bradford in 1904. Bradford was one of the city's most active and prosperous real estate men at the turn of the twentieth century. He studied at Heidelberg and Stuttgart Universities and at the École des Beaux-Arts in Paris. After returning to the United States and traveling throughout the West, he moved to Washington, D.C., and worked as an architect until he went into the real estate business in 1884. One of his larger deals was the sale of the Westmoreland apartments (2100 block of California Street) by the Highlands Company in 1907. Bradford was found dead at his office in November 1914 at the age of fifty-five. In 1920, the house became the home of the Armenian Legation, and it is now the embassy of the Gabonese Republic.

Alvin Lothrop Mansion (2001 Connecticut Avenue)

Samuel Woodward's business partner, Alvin Lothrop, built his grand, Beaux-Arts–style mansion at 2001 Connecticut Avenue on the former location of the Tindall house in 1909. It was designed by the local architectural firm Hornblower & Marshall, recognized for its skill in the Beaux-Arts style that became popular in Washington in the late 1890s.

While planning their new home, the Lothrops experienced great personal tragedy with the death of their daughter Caroline in October 1908. Then, in early 1909, Mrs. Lothrop was stricken with an incurable form of arthritis and also died. In that year, Lothrop, now a widower, moved into the new mansion with his college-age daughter, Harriet. The house served as Lothrop's home for only a short time.

During his brief residence in the house, Lothrop probably did not spend a lot of time there. After the death of his wife, he divided much of his time between his childhood home of South Acton, Massachusetts, and his summer place, Camp Kanosa, in the Adirondack Mountains. Lothrop died within three years of taking up residence in the house. He had suffered from Bright's disease, but his unexpected death in 1912 was due to a stroke.

The Lothrop Mansion at 2001 Connecticut Avenue, circa 1915. The apartment building at 2029 Connecticut Avenue can be seen under construction to the right. *Courtesy Library of Congress, Prints and Photographs Division.*

Alvin Lothrop, co-founder of Woodward and Lothrop Department Store. *Courtesy of the Washingtoniana Room, Martin Luther King Library.*

Lothrop's daughter Harriet, who had married Nathaniel Horace Luttrell, was living at 2132 Bancroft Place NW when she died suddenly on February 15, 1919. While the cause of her death was unlisted, she may have been one of Washington's thousands of victims to be stricken by the Spanish flu epidemic that ravaged the world for two years. After her death, Nathan Luttrell and his children moved into the Lothrop mansion. The mansion was later purchased by the Soviet government and used as the chancellery of the embassy, and it is now the office of the Trade Representative of the Russian Federation. It was listed on the National Register of Historic Places in 1988.

Lothrop's grandson, Alvin Lothrop Luttrell, joined Woodward & Lothrop in 1938 and became a director in 1942. He was elected executive vice-president in 1947 and chairman of the board's executive committee in 1961. He served as board chairman from 1965 until retiring in 1978.

Architects James Rush Marshall and Joseph Coerten Hornblower worked together for over thirty years as the firm of Hornblower & Marshall. Their work included the new National History Museum Building, the Army and Navy Club and private residences in Washington and the United States Custom House in Baltimore. Their only other work in Kalorama Triangle was a pair of relatively modest town houses at 2504–6 Cliffbourne Place, which they designed in 1899.

TRUESDELL'S ESTATE (WIDOW'S MITE)

Perhaps no one person had as much influence on the development of Kalorama Triangle as did George Truesdell. Truesdell was born in 1842 in Fairmount, New York, and was a Civil War veteran, having been commissioned as a major and paymaster in the army. Before arriving in Washington in 1872, he had worked as a civil engineer in New Jersey. Upon his arrival in Washington, Truesdell immediately started buying and selling land. In the 1880s, he bought fifteen acres of Widow's Mite from the real estate firm Davidson & Davidson.

Colonel George Truesdell, real estate speculator, developer and District commissioner. *Courtesy Library of Congress, Prints and Photographs Division.*

On part of his land fronting on Columbia Road, Truesdell built his less-than-modest summer home, Managasset. He subdivided the remaining part of the land in 1887 as Truesdell's Addition to Washington Heights. A year after creating the subdivision, he organized the District's first electric streetcar railway, the Eckington and Soldiers' Home Railway Company. The city's second electric railway, the Rock Creek Railway, was chartered only a month later, with Truesdell serving as its president.

George Truesdell's summer home, Managasset, once stood on Columbia Road. *Courtesy the Historical Society of Washington, D.C.*

Truesdell served as a District commissioner from 1894 to 1897 while the commission itself was considering routing the extension of Connecticut Avenue through his own property. He also served with neighbor Samuel Woodward as vice-chair of the committee of the Washington Sanitary Housing Company. In the 1890s, Truesdell would begin to sell parts of his own estate in Widow's Mite, lot by lot, until 1911, when he would finally demolish Managasset to build the Altamont apartment building.

In 1896, Truesdell cut his Widow's Mite estate in half by donating 16,200 square feet of ground to the District for the extension of Twentieth Street. The *Washington Post* stated that "although this land is very valuable, the Commissioner has given it to the public simply because he realizes the importance of opening Twentieth Street."[42] Although this was seen as a charitable act at the time, Truesdell would have probably been required to have done the same under the Highway Act of 1893. Additionally, this created new street frontage on his property that he would then be able to divide into house lots. Truesdell knew that whoever built on these lots would be close neighbors and that their houses would be visible from his Managasset. Not surprisingly, the new lots were large, intended to attract wealthier buyers.

Colonel Charles H. Heyl (2009 Wyoming Avenue)

One of Truesdell's first sales of house lots in Widow's Mite was to Lieutenant Colonel Charles Heyl in 1898 at 2009 Wyoming Avenue. Colonel Heyl was awarded the Medal of Honor for attacking six Indians near Fort Hartsuff, Nebraska, in 1876. The house, which still stands today, although greatly modified, was designed by architect L. Norris.

Colonel Charles Heath Heyl. *Courtesy Library of Congress, Prints and Photographs Division.*

Heyl's house is similar to the one designed the same year by Waddy Wood for Dr. Arthur Keith at 2210 Twentieth Street. At first glance, these houses appear to be either the first or the last in a planned series of town houses. But by minimizing the street frontage and maximizing the building's depth, Norris was able to take advantage of the long side of the house, adding windows set back a distance from the façade and street, offering both sunlight and privacy.

Dr. Arthur Keith (2210 Twentieth Street)

The first lot Truesdell sold on his new block of Twentieth Street was number 2210. The house was designed for Dr. Arthur Keith by architect Waddy Butler Wood in 1898, the same year as Colonel Heyl's house on Wyoming Avenue. Here, Wood also embellished the long side elevation with a Palladian window, a popular Georgian Revival feature.

Dr. Arthur Keith's house at 2210 Twentieth Street was designed by noted architect Waddy Butler Wood. *Photo by the author.*

Arthur Keith was a geologist and served as a president of the Geological Society of America. After graduating from Harvard, Keith went directly into geologic fieldwork, first with the Massachusetts Topographic Survey. In 1887, he moved to Washington and became an early member of the Federal Survey. He was elected to the Geological Society of America in 1889, only one year after it was founded.

Keith was still a bachelor and living with his mother, Mrs. Mary R. Keith, when he had his house built. She continued to live with him until her death in 1916. In her will, she directed that a fund of $2,500 be held in trust for her son, with the remainder of the estate devised to him with the explanation that he is a "scientist by profession, which does not, as a rule, pay very liberally."[43] In 1916, Keith married Elizabeth Mary Smith of Athens, Ohio. They had no children. Elizabeth worked with him in preparing his publications and often went with him into the field. She was his close companion until her death in 1942. After a long illness, Arthur Keith passed away in Silver Spring, Maryland, in 1944. Over the front doorway of the house is now a keystone featuring a relief of Arthur Keith.

The Mendota: Kalorama Triangle's First Apartment Building

In 1901, George Truesdell sold a plot of land on which his greenhouse had once stood at the southwest corner of Kalorama Road and Twentieth Street to the Iowa Apartment House Company. On this lot, the first apartment building in Kalorama Triangle, the Mendota, a Sioux Indian word meaning "mouth of the river," was constructed at 2220 Twentieth Street and opened in 1902.

The Mendota was the first of three apartment buildings designed by James G. Hill, the others being Stoneleigh Court and the Ontario.

Built in 1901, the Mendota was the first apartment building in Kalorama Triangle. *Courtesy the Historical Society of Washington, D.C.*

Mendota resident Jeanette Rankin was the first woman elected to Congress and the only member of Congress to vote against the United States entering World War II. *Courtesy Library of Congress, Prints and Photographs Division.*

When built, the Mendota had forty-nine apartments: twenty-three one-bedrooms, twelve two-bedrooms, seven three-bedrooms and seven four-bedrooms. For those who chose not to cook or did not have their domestic staff with them, the top floor featured a public dining room. The ground floor contained a drugstore and a doctor's office. Prominent residents of the Mendota included its architect, James Hill, Kalorama developer Lawrence Sands and Sands's wife, Margaret Foyle Sands, who was one of the daughters of John Little. The Mendota was also home to progressive Nebraska senator George W. Norris and Jeanette Rankin, the first woman to serve in Congress. The book *A Single Woman* is based on her life and was made into a film in 2008. The Mendota was converted to a co-op in 1952.

Taft Bridge Inn (2007 Wyoming Avenue)

Next door to Colonel Heyl's house on Wyoming Avenue, the two-story brick and stone house at number 2007 (now the Taft Bridge Inn) was built in 1905 for local contractor Lewis E. Smoot and designed by architect Thomas J.D. Fuller.

While the house was being built, Smoot requested that the inspector of buildings visit the premises and set a party wall between his and Heyl's lots. A party wall is a shared structural wall between two town

Architect Thomas J.D. Fuller designed this house for Lewis E. Smoot at 2007 Wyoming Avenue in 1905. *Photo by the author.*

houses on which they are both built. The building regulations governing party walls were established during George Washington's presidency and had not been changed since. The inspector refused to visit the site, perhaps because he thought that a party wall was not needed between two freestanding houses. Smoot sued in an attempt to have the court force the inspector to comply with the request. But Smoot's party wall was never built. In 1913, Smooth added a bay window partially on his neighbor Colonel Heyl's lot, claiming that it served as a party wall and that Washington's original regulations allowed it. The case went to the Supreme Court, as it challenged the constitutional validity of the original building regulations. In Smoot's case, the Supreme Court determined that George Washington never intended that a bay window should be considered a party wall.

This was not the only time an issue over a party wall in Kalorama Triangle went all the way to the Supreme Court. In 1916, Genevieve K. Gish, the owner of 2327 Ashmead Place, sued developer Ernest Walker for $150.00 for nonpayment for the use of her party wall when he built the adjoining set of houses at 2329–31 Ashmead Place. Gish won and was awarded $144.63. Walker appealed the decision, and the case was active for seven years and was finally argued in front of the Supreme Court in 1923. William Howard Taft, then chief justice of the Supreme Court, wrote the opinion ruling in favor of Miss Gish.

Charlotte Dailey (2200 Twentieth Street)

Immediately to the right and back of 2007 Wyoming is the grand house at 2200 Twentieth Street. Built in 1906 for owner Charlotte Manning Dailey, the house was a collaborative effort between Charlotte Dailey and the team of architect Albert H. Beers and builder Harry Wardman. Dailey, Wardman and Beers worked together on several other projects. Dailey would acquire the land, and Wardman and Beers would provide the building. Their projects included the Belgrade at Eighteenth Street and Florida, which she sold to real estate and hotel magnate Orrin G. Staples. Staples, in turn, bought another Dailey-Beers-Wardman house at 1825 Columbia Road in 1911.

Charlotte Dailey was one of the wealthiest and most prominent society women in Washington at the time. Barely a year in her new house, she alleged that her husband, William F. Dailey, was a cocaine addict, a drunkard and abusive and sued for divorce in 1907. Charlotte also suffered from severe

Home of Charlotte Dailey at 2200 Twentieth Street. *Photo by the author.*

depression, and in 1914, she ended her life. She had fastened a gas tube attached to a chandelier fixture in her mouth and turned the gas on. She was found, sitting in a Morris chair in her bedroom, by her chauffer.

In her will, she placed her estate in trust with the American Security and Trust Company, with a provision that her maid, Mary E. Brown, was to receive a life annuity of $35 a month. Upon her death, the income would then go to Charlotte's only daughter, Rita Childress, and eventually to her daughter's children for twenty-one years. Rita contested the will, claiming that her mother had been mentally incompetent to make a valid will. In 1917, a jury ruled in Rita's favor, and she acquired her mother's entire $150,000 estate. Rita and her husband, John W. Childress, took occupancy of the house.

John Childress was a real estate developer, and in 1926, President Calvin Coolidge appointed him the first head of the Public Utilities Commission for the District, but he resigned in 1929 to become a general agent for the United States Steamship Lines. In 1933, along with Kalorama Triangle builder Ernest G. Walker, Childress was in the running for an appointment by President Franklin D. Roosevelt as a District commissioner, though neither man received the appointment. The two Childress daughters, Adair and Charlotte, became high-profile Washington society debutantes.

In 1916, the Childresses rented space in the house for use as a private piano studio. They also opened their house to the Home of Truth religious movement, a precursor of the New Thought movement and the Divine Science Church. The movement believed, among other things, that the spirit is the totality of real things and sickness originates in the mind.[44] In 1935, one of the founders of the Home of Truth, Marie Ogden, had kept the dead body of a female member for almost two years in Utah, contending that she was still "spiritually alive" and was attempting to restore physical life. While not willing to discuss the case further with the press, she did admit to "making satisfactory progress."[45]

With his wife and his youngest daughter Adair in Europe and his other daughter Charlotte visiting friends on the North Shore, in August 1929, John Childress threw a stag party probably unrivaled in Kalorama Triangle at that time or for years to come. The *Washington Post* reported that the "Good Ship Friendship" set sail that night, with Mr. John Childress as the "skipper" and a distinguished list of passengers aboard. At the time, Childress was general agent of the United States Steamship Lines, and party guests included officials of the Shipping Board and steamship and railroad passenger agents from Washington, Baltimore and Richmond. Throwing Prohibition to the wind, the invitations were printed on blue paper with an ocean liner at the top and read:

> *You are cordially invited to the special sailing of the Good Ship Friendship. The ship sails from 2200 Twentieth Street, Washington, DC on August 3, 1929, at 8 o'clock sharp (midnight wasting time). Galley and open bar open immediately after leaving the dock—well within the 12-mile limit. Your embarkation card is attached. Signed, John W. Childress*[46]

The Childresses had left the house by 1940. By 1945, the house had become the local headquarters of the Women of Moose Club. Later, it became home to Women's City Club, which held its annual rummage sales there. Mrs. Herbert Hoover was one of the club's first members. In 1964, it celebrated its forty-fifth anniversary at the house. It may have been just coincidence or New Thought metaphysical principles in action, but in 1971, the First Divine Science Church returned to the house, and it served as their church until 1976.

John Childress died in 1963 at the age of eighty-four. At the time of his death, he, Rita and daughter Mrs. J.O. Urquhart were living at 3701 Oliver Street NW.

The Altamont

In 1911, Truesdell started planning to build a new home for himself. That year, he accepted bids for construction of a $100,000 house on the corner of Wyoming and Twentieth Streets, the site of his current home, Managasset. The proposal was for a building of brick and stone finish and steel and concrete construction, three and a half stories in height. But at the same time, the Washington Heights Citizen's Association was attempting to acquire Managasset and its grounds for use as a public nursery and playgrounds. Neither plan succeeded. Truesdell's new house was never built on the property, nor did it become a nursery and playgrounds. Managasset was ultimately razed to make way for Truesdell's new plan for the site, the Altamont apartment building, where he took up residence after his home Managasset was razed.

The Altamont was named after the Truesdells' 1,500-acre summer home, a converted barn near Deep Creek Lake, Maryland. Deep Creek was a fashionable summer resort for many years where President Cleveland took

George Truesdell razed his summer home, Managasset, to construct the Altamont apartment building in 1911. *Courtesy Library of Congress, Prints and Photographs Division.*

his bride for their honeymoon. Truesdell's home boasted a view over the tops of the Allegheny Mountains and was the source of Altamont Spring water, which he owned. The Truesdells spent every summer at their home near Deep Creek Lake, and in later years, they began to occupy Managasset only rarely in the winter months, preferring their other home near his other subdivision, Eckington, in Northeast Washington, D.C.

The Altamont was designed by Arthur B. Heaton in the very popular Mission Revival style and was completed in 1916. Heaton designed twenty-eight apartment buildings between 1900 and 1940, including the Highland apartment building at 1914 Connecticut Avenue in 1902. Heaton served as the first supervising architect on the construction of the Washington Cathedral between 1908 and 1928.

When it opened, the Altamont contained twenty-seven apartments: four efficiencies, fourteen one-bedroom, three two-bedroom and six four-bedroom apartments. The top of the building provided a complete escape from the streets below, with two summer pavilions on the roof and a dining room. The basement contained a billiard room, a barbershop, a beauty parlor, a servants' dining room and a laundry room. The Altamont was converted to a co-op in 1949.

In planning both the Mendota and the Altamont, Truesdell provided commercial services for the occupants. The Mendota's drugstore and doctor's office, and the Altamont's barbershop and beauty parlor, teamed with the Mendota Market (now a 7-11), provided a range of services and food items to residents of the Mendota and the Altamont. The owner of the Mendota Market was well aware of the affluence of his local customers, and in 1918, an unfair food order was issued by the city's food administrator against its owner, W.B. Krantz, prohibiting all licensed food distributors from engaging in any business with him.

Apartment Buildings for the Middle Class

The 1920s saw a rise in the demand for middle-class housing in Kalorama Triangle. With Truesdell's Managasset estate now gone and the Altamont already constructed, the block still provided ample room for new middle-class apartment buildings. The first of these buildings, the Montello at 1901 Columbia Road, was built in 1921. The Montello signifies a break in design from the earlier, more ornate apartment buildings already built in Kalorama Triangle. It was designed by architect Frank Russell White and built by Ernest George Walker. Like Harry Wardman, White specialized in apartment buildings for those of more modest means. He was a prolific architect, and in addition to working with Christian Heurich and Franklin T. Sanner, after the death of Beers, he worked with Harry Wardman in building about 266 houses and apartment buildings between 1910 and 1918.

In 1923, builder Ernest Walker erected three more apartment buildings surrounding the Altamont between Nineteenth Street and Kalorama and Twentieth Street. The tallest and most architecturally detailed building, now the Shawmut, fronted on Nineteenth Street. The Woburn fronted on Kalorama Road, and the Knowlton was on Twentieth Street, across from the Mendota. The Knowlton may have been named for Grace Knowlton, the wife of Kalorama Triangle architect Clarke Waggaman.

Washington builder Ernest George Walker was one of the premier builders in Kalorama Triangle. In addition to the apartment buildings on Truesdell's estate, Walker was selected by architects Reginald Wyckliffe Geare and Matthew G. Lepley to build in the popular Mission Revival style that was sweeping the neighborhood.

The Knowlton at 2227 Twentieth Street was built in 1923 and was one of three apartment buildings on the block intended for mostly middle-class occupants. *Courtesy of the Washingtoniana Room, Martin Luther King Library.*

The Mission Revival style in Kalorama Triangle was an eclectic style drawn from various phases of Spanish Colonial architecture that was popular in the United States from about 1890 to 1920. Distinguishing elements of the Mission Revival style include stucco-finished or light-colored brick walls, Flemish gables, rows of round arched windows, iron balconies or balconets in front of windows on the second floor, red tile roofs with large overhangs and exposed rafters.

LITTLE'S SUBDIVISION

In 1880, John Little's five daughters subdivided their property lying to the east of Columbia Road, from its southern tip at Columbia and Nineteenth Street north to Biltmore Street, into nine lots. In 1884, Lawrence Sands and his wife, John Little's daughter Margaret Foyle Sands, subdivided three of these lots, creating the Mintwood subdivision centered on Mintwood

Place. Mintwood divided the Little holdings along Columbia Road into two sections. One section consisted of what is now Kalorama Park; the other section ran north from Mintwood Place to Biltmore Street providing valuable frontage on Columbia Road.

In 1888, the Littles and multiple other stakeholders subdivided their holdings to the east of Columbia Road, which became known as the Commissioner's subdivision. The year 1903 marked the final sale of what remained of the Little estate. By then, the estate had been reduced to only the triangular area covered by what is now Kalorama Park and was divided between Little's daughters Ida Little Stevens and Finella Alexander. Ida Little Stevens had died earlier that year, and in November, Finella Alexander sold the northern half of the land, including the Little house, to Thomas W. Smith. Smith was a prominent lumber merchant and former president of the Board of Trade and the Chamber of Commerce. The following month, Ida Little's estate put the southern section of the triangle up for auction.

The southern section was bought by German immigrant, brewer and real estate magnate Christian Heurich. Heurich's purchase had a frontage of 288 feet on Columbia Road and 480 feet on Nineteenth Street. Heurich worked with architect Appleton P. Clark and planned to construct the largest apartment building to date in the city, but the Highway Act of 1898 required the connection of the two separate ends of Kalorama Road through the property, thwarting Heurich's plans for his apartment building. In 1926, Heurich sold his part of the Little property to the Alonzo O. Bliss Properties Trust. Bliss's son Arthur L. Bliss would eventually purchase the Woodward apartment building.

Thomas Smith died in March 1919, leaving his various properties in a trust with the Washington Loan and Trust Company. He left the house to his wife, Caroline, for the duration of her life, but she decided not to remain there. By 1919, Samuel Jordan Graham, former attorney general under President Wilson and then judge of the United States Court of Claims, was renting the Little house from the Smith trust and was living there with his wife and daughter Mary. By 1927, the Little house had become a boardinghouse.

The Little Farm Becomes Kalorama Park

The first park in Kalorama Triangle was the small reservation or triangle at the intersection of Kalorama Road, Columbia Road and Nineteenth Street, created when the two parts of Kalorama Road were connected in 1904. But

Kalorama Park. *Photo by the author.*

this did not afford much space for the number of children who needed a decent-sized place to play.

In 1906, the Washington Heights Citizens Association was formed around the issue of creating a larger park. George Truesdell was on the organizational committee, and Thomas J.D. Fuller and Samuel Woodward were appointed to the park committee. But by 1911, there still was not a new park, and residents were complaining that the area along Columbia Road and adjacent streets was now a "congested district." There were ten thousand people living in the immediate vicinity and more than three thousand babies. The closest outdoor public areas were either Dupont Circle or the zoo.

Aware that Truesdell rarely used his summer home, the Washington Heights Citizens Association asked the District commissioners to turn Truesdell's property into a park. Managasset would be used as a nursery, with the lawns to be turned into playgrounds. The property was valued at $250,000. The commission appointed a committee to put together a proposal combining federal, District and private funds to acquire the land. The plan was ultimately rejected by the commission, as many thought that other areas were in much more need of a public nursery than the wealthier residents of Kalorama. Truesdell kept his land, and Managasset became the site for his new Altamont apartment building.

In 1942, the National Capital Park and Planning Commission acquired the northern part of the property from the Smith Trust. The Little House had already disappeared by this time. That year, it was named Kalorama Park in recognition of the Kalorama Citizens Association's (formerly the Washington Heights Citizens Association) role in procuring the park. In 1946, the Alonzo Bliss Properties Trust deeded the southern part of the property to the United States government, at which point the two parts of the Little property were once again joined and the land was added to the park. In 2010, the northern three-quarters of the park became the Kalorama Park Archaeological Site and was designated a D.C. historic landmark.

Columbia Road: From a Residential to a Commercial District

Surprisingly, the Littles' lots that ran north along well-traveled Columbia Road sat vacant for twenty-five years. Finally, in 1905, the team of Albert Beers and Harry Wardman built three sets of matching duplex town houses at 1813–15 and 1817–19 Columbia Road and 1822–24 Biltmore Street. The pair of houses on Biltmore is still standing.

In 1907, Wardman and Beers built another house at 1825 Columbia Road for railroad contractor Hollis J. Rinehart and his family. It was purchased by hotel magnate Colonel Orrin G. Staples in 1911.

Orrin Staples was born in 1851 in Watertown, New York. He began his successful hotel career in 1872, when he built the Thousand Island House in Alexandria Bay on the St. Lawrence River. A year later, he sold the hotel and moved to Washington. In Washington, Staples bought the old Willard Hotel and, in 1891, the Riggs House hotel, located at Fifteenth and G Streets, where he lived until purchasing the Columbia Road house in 1911. In 1895, Staples sold the Willard, only to buy it back two years later when the purchaser lost the property under foreclosure. Staples sold the property again in 1899 to a syndicate that subsequently built the grand New Willard hotel that is there today.

Anticipating the demand for business properties along the west side of Columbia Road, John Henry from Brooklyn, New York, bought the Staples house in 1922. He intended to build two substantial business buildings on the site that would benefit a rapidly growing neighborhood as soon as the block was rezoned for commercial use. The east side of Columbia Road already allowed commercial use.

But the District commissioners held out, refusing to rezone the 1800 block of Columbia Road between Mintwood Place and Biltmore Street from

Above: The duplex town houses at 1822–24 Biltmore Street were built by Harry Wardman in 1905. These were originally one of a set of three such town houses. The others once stood at 1817 and 1819 Columbia Road but were razed in 1929 to make way for shops. *Photo by the author.*

Below: The home of Orrin G. Staples once stood at 1825 Columbia Road. Photo circa 1911. *Courtesy Library of Congress, Prints and Photographs Division.*

strictly residential to commercial use. The partial block between Biltmore Street and Adams Mill Road did not have any building or use restrictions and had already been developed for commercial use by Franklin T. Sanner and Harry Wardman.

Then, in 1929, the commissioners finally decided to change the zoning regulations to allow commercial use of the block. As a result of the rezoning, the block changed dramatically. Colonel George L. Andrews's house at 1847 Columbia Road was razed to erect the mixed-use Mintwood apartment building. That year, Wardman's houses along Columbia road began to be razed to be replaced by a series of one-story storefront buildings, as well as the two-story building at 1811 Columbia Road (now Perry's Restaurant), designed by the architect of Cliffbourne's Painted Ladies, Frederick Pyle, in 1929.

Biltmore Street

The Little subdivision also encompassed the southern side of the 1800 and 1900 blocks of Biltmore Street until it intersects with Nineteenth Street. The 1900 block was the first to be divided into house lots, and a total of seventeen town houses were built in 1902 by developer Lester Barr and architect B. Stanley Simmons, designer of the Wyoming apartment building. The 1800 block would be divided later into larger lots that lent themselves to larger freestanding houses, town homes and apartment buildings.

Harry Wardman and Arthur Beers continued their work on Biltmore, but not together. The four-story Baltimore apartment building at 1832 Biltmore was built in 1905 by Wardman, but he chose to work with architect N.R. Grimm, who designed the Cliffbourne at 1915 Calvert Street that same year. In 1910, Beers designed a two-story brick house with a one-story wooden porch at 1826 Biltmore Street.

In addition to the Baltimore, the western half of the block is home to two other large apartment buildings: the Haddington at 1840 Biltmore, built by Berkley L. Simmons and designed by George N. Ray (1912); and 1900 Biltmore Street, designed by Frank White (1922), who also designed the Rockledge apartment building at 2456 Twentieth Street.

The southern part of the 1800 block of Biltmore Street is also home to several large, elegant town houses. Here, architects were given license and budgets to experiment with popular styles. Examples include the town house at 1848 Biltmore that was designed in 1909 by the

Altamont's architect, Arthur B. Heaton, where he combined a mixture of Mediterranean and Georgian Revival styles. The two Mediterranean-influenced houses at 1850 and 1852 Biltmore Street were built in 1911 by architect and builder W. Granville Guss. Number 1852 Biltmore is very distinguishable, with its unique geometric door surround that steps back in successively smaller plans. Next door, the Jacobean Revival–style house at 1854 Biltmore Street was designed by architects Gregg and Leisenring in 1912.

SANDS'S SUBDIVISION

In 1878, Lawrence Sands, a wealthy attorney and former president of the First-Second National Bank of Pittsburgh, married John Little's daughter Margaret Foyle Sands. The couple, along with Margaret's sisters Sophia and Finella, would become partners in subdividing and selling off the Little estate for development.

The northern part of the 1900 block of Belmont in Sands's subdivision has experienced three successive development phases. It was initially the site of two large mansions in the 1880s and then became home to a hotel and low-income rental housing in the 1960s before becoming a town house development in the 1990s.

Lawrence Sands built his country mansion, Mintwood, on part of the Little estate on the 1900 block of Belmont (then Woodley Lane) in 1883. It was the largest house in Kalorama at that time, built of brick with three stories and thirty rooms.

In 1885, Sands subdivided his property where his Mintwood home stood into two lots. He sold the western lot to Samuel S. Shedd, a successful Washington plumber, who built a large, wood-frame, Queen Anne–style house next to Sands's house, at the corner of present-day Belmont Road and Twentieth Street. Shedd chose for his builders the firm of Langley & Gettinger, which had also built Sands's Mintwood estate.

Shedd was in the plumbing business for more than thirty years. His firm, S.S. Shedd & Bro. Co., was located on Ninth Street downtown. Shedd eventually sold the house to Henry Pierpont Waggaman and moved to Takoma Park, Maryland, where he served as mayor between 1894 and 1902.

Henry Pierpont Waggaman was born in Fairfax County, Virginia, in 1845 and was the brother of Kalorama Triangle developer Thomas Ennalls Waggaman and Woodley Park developer and Rock Creek Railway board

Above: Kalorama Triangle developer Lawrence Sands's house, Mintwood, once stood in the 1900 block of Belmont Road. *Courtesy of the Washingtoniana Room, Martin Luther King Library.*

Below: Samuel Shedd's house on the 1900 block of Belmont Road. *Courtesy of the Washingtoniana Room, Martin Luther King Library.*

member John Floyd Waggaman. During the Civil War, Henry joined the Confederate army, fought at the Battle of Bull Run and was later injured in a battle in Virginia as a member of the Sixth Virginia Cavalry. Along with his brothers, he became involved in real estate development.

In 1905, in relation to the cases against his brother Thomas Waggaman, Catholic University filed suits against Henry Waggaman and his brother John seeking to recover over $100,000 in promissory notes and interest. In 1907, Henry Waggaman was sued by his late brother Thomas's estate to recover $1 million in promissory notes made to Thomas. But Henry had left Washington and moved to New York in 1901.

Lawrence Sands sold his Mintwood estate in 1904, which included the house together with seventy-one thousand square feet of land, to William J. Kehoe for $100,000. Sands and his wife, Margaret, moved to the recently built Mendota apartment building. On the far end of the Sands estate at 1940 Biltmore Street, Joseph J. Moebs, builder of the Beacon apartments on Calvert Street in 1910, erected the Biltmore apartment building in 1913.

A Tale of Two Schools

In 1902, the Chevy Chase School for Girls, a French and English boarding school for young ladies located in Chevy Chase, bought the Waggaman house on Belmont Road and opened a Washington campus for the school. Miss Bristol's School, which had been operating out of a town house at 1865 Mintwood Place, then moved to the Sands mansion next door. Miss Bristol's School was also a boarding and day school for girls, but boys were admitted to kindergarten and primary levels. The school offered "unusual advantages" in the piano department for young ladies.

In 1905, the two schools were combined, with Miss Alice Bristol serving as principal. The Bristol School advertised itself as an Episcopal school for girls, offering primary, intermediate, preparatory and collegiate courses. The Chevy Chase School, now the Chevy Chase house, became the French residence for the school, where French was spoken from 7:00 a.m. to 5:00 p.m. offering advantages in language training equal to a residence abroad.

In 1910, William Kehoe, who bought the Sands estate, erected a new three-story building on the site for the Bristol School. Known as Collegiate Hall, it contained an assembly hall, classrooms, a library, a gymnasium and a department of home economics. To the north of the campus, Studio Hall was added, a fireproof building containing sixty-five rooms and baths.

In 1911, the Bristol School bought an additional twenty-two thousand square feet at Twentieth and Belmont to occupy the entire square and create a campus with gardens, trees and a large athletic field for the school. In 1920, the Bristol School was purchased by Dr. Arthur Ramsay, and it became the Fairmont Seminary. Ramsay took the former Waggaman house as his private residence.

The Fairmont Seminary was founded by Dr. Ramsey in 1898 and had previously occupied a building at Fourteenth and Euclid Streets and a residence on Clifton Street. Like the Bristol School, it emphasized the arts and was reputed to be one of the District's best finishing schools for girls. One student, Agnes Hannah Kurowsky, met Ernest Hemingway in Italy in 1918 and was the inspiration for *A Farewell to Arms*, although in real life Agnes apparently did not share Hemingway's feelings for her. The school continued operation until 1943, when it was "closed for the duration."

The Sand and Shedd mansions were razed to make way for the Rock Creek Hotel and affordable apartment buildings in the 1960s. Thirty years later, the entire site was again razed for the present-day Kalorama Place town house development.

MINTWOOD SUBDIVISION

In 1884, Lawrence and Margaret Sands created the Mintwood subdivision out of several lots from the Little estate. Mintwood became a form of family-owned corporation, with the other Little sisters buying and selling lots within the division.

In 1891, Colonel George L. Andrews acquired a large lot in the Mintwood subdivision at 1847 Columbia Road, where he constructed a large Queen Anne–style house. Andrew's house, designed by T.F. Schneider, who would also design the Woodley apartment building next door, had the newest technologies, including steam heat, and was wired for electric lights. Electric lighting was slow to catch on, with many believing that it was more of a fire risk than gas. Up until the 1920s, many homes were built with both.

Andrews was a Rhode Island native. He served in 1861 as lieutenant colonel of the First Missouri Infantry and was wounded at the Battle of Wilson's Creek, Missouri. Andrews continued to serve in various departmental adjutant roles from 1908 to August 1912, when he was promoted to adjutant general of the U.S. Army with the rank of brigadier

Above: George L. Andrews's house at 1847 Columbia Road. The site of the house is now the Mintwood apartment building. *Courtesy of the Washingtoniana Room, Martin Luther King Library.*

Left: Brigadier General Colonel George L. Andrews. *Courtesy Library of Congress, Prints and Photographs Division.*

general. He retired in August 1914 and died in 1928 in Washington, D.C. He is buried in Arlington National Cemetery. The house was razed in 1929, and the location is now occupied by the Mintwood apartment building.

The Woodley (1851 Columbia Road)

The Woodley apartment building, located at 1851 Columbia Road, was constructed in 1903 for the Woodley Apartment House Company, which had incorporated in Alexandria, Virginia, with Samuel W. Woodward as its president. It was the first apartment building constructed on Columbia Road and was designed by one of Washington's prominent architects, Thomas Franklin Schneider. In 1894, Schneider had designed the Cairo Flats (now the Cairo Condominiums) at 1615 Q Street NW, which is still the second-tallest building in Washington, D.C., after the Washington Monument. The Cairo was nicknamed Schneider's Folly, and protests against its height led Congress to pass the Heights of Buildings Act of

The Woodley at 1851 Columbia Road was built in 1903 and was the first apartment building on Columbia Road. *Courtesy the Historical Society of Washington, D.C.*

1910. While not under any building height restrictions in 1903 and not reaching the Cairo's height, the Woodley also stood out with its singular height on Columbia Road.

The construction of the Woodley had its share of problems. Schneider was given a stop-work order and had his permit revoked for failing to remove condemned property from in front of the construction site, though he continued construction. The condemned materials were probably the remains of a small house that was part of the Little estate that stood on the construction site of the Woodley.

The alleged employment of non-union tile workers by the Woodley's builder, Duehay & Sons, led labor leaders Allied Building Trades to order all workmen on the site to stop work on the building, along with three other Schneider apartment buildings also under construction by Duehay & Sons. On November 5, 1903, a total of 250 workers walked off their jobs.

When finally completed, the Woodley boasted only six spacious apartments on each floor. It was touted as one of the most complete apartment houses in Washington Heights, with seven stories, fireproof construction and forty-two three- to six-room apartments, all elaborately decorated. The exterior is elaborate, with an imposing entrance and porte-cochere.

The Garden T Shoppe was located on the ground floor of the Mintwood Apartments at 1845 Columbia Road. Other shops in the building included a laundry and Gildenhorn's Market. Photo circa 1937. *Courtesy Library of Congress, Prints and Photographs Division.*

In 1929, the zoning on the west side of Columbia Road between Mintwood Place and Biltmore Street changed from strictly residential to allow commercial use. That year, the Mintwood Corporation bought the site of the Andrews house from Washington theater owner Harry Crandall and erected the Mintwood apartment building. The Mintwood was an eight-story, mixed-use apartment house and contained 121 apartments, with stores on the first floor at 1845 Columbia Road. The building was sold three years later at a loss, likely another casualty of the Depression.

1850 Mintwood Place

The earliest and best-known house on Mintwood Place is located at 1850 Mintwood, built in 1898 and designed for Mary McAllister by architect Waddy Wood. Wood began working with McAllister in 1896 when McAllister commissioned him to build three buildings at 1792–96 Columbia Road and a house at 2110 G Street in Foggy Bottom the following year. The house on Mintwood Place was their third project together and Wood's first work in the Arts and Crafts style. In 1899, they would collaborate once more on an Arts and Crafts–style building at

The Arts and Crafts–style house at 1850 Mintwood Place was designed by Waddy Wood in 1898. *Photo by the author.*

2481 Eighteenth Street that once was a People's Drug Store and is now a McDonald's restaurant.

The Craftsman style of the Arts and Crafts movement, as embraced by Wood, abandoned traditional American architectural precedents by using Tudor-style stucco and exposed half-timbers, large overhanging timbered eaves with exposed rafters and often tracery-patterned and diagonally set windowpanes. For the house at 1850 Mintwood Place, Wood was influenced by Thomas Fuller's use of the English Free Style for his home at 2317 Ashmead Place. Whereas Fuller had chosen an overall Georgian theme for his house, Wood selected the Tudor style. On the first floor, Wood used oversized yellow brick, a contemporary interpretation of arched stone window surrounds embellished with prominent keystones and stone corner quoins. The second floor provides a contrast in textures and color to the first floor with stucco and exposed half-timbers in the gabled dormers.

Town Houses on Mintwood Place

The first town house built on Mintwood Place was at 1842 Mintwood. Introducing the Georgian Revival style in Kalorama, this house was built for H.W. Fuller and designed by architect Peter Walter in 1898. It was originally built as a single residence and was added onto in 1900.

Most of the town houses on Mintwood Place were built on speculation between 1898 and 1906. Five town houses were built in 1899 by Metcalf & Lewis and designed by architect B. Stanley Simmons, who also designed the 1900 block of Biltmore Street. Franklin T. Sanner constructed ten town houses between 1901 and 1904. In 1904, he would build his own house at 1808 Adams Mill Road. That same year, Lester A. Barr constructed six houses, and in 1906, architect and builder George S. Cooper, who built the first row houses in Presbrey and Goddard's subdivision in 1899, built the last two town houses on the street.

Mintwood Place's Apartment Buildings

The momentum to build town houses on Mintwood Place was replaced with the construction of apartment buildings starting in 1909. The Knickerbocker apartment building at 1840 Mintwood Place was built in 1909 by Howard Etchison. The four-story apartment building at 1869 Mintwood, built by Berkeley L. Simmons in 1916, was intended to give the appearance of a large single residence.

The apartment building at 1875 Mintwood Place was built in 1925 by Harry M. Bralove and designed by George T. Santmyers. Two years later, Bralove and Santmyers, in collaboration with architect Joseph Abel, would build 2101 Connecticut Avenue. The Gothic Revival–style entranceway and Georgian-style quoined corners of 1875 Mintwood Place foreshadow the eclectic use of architectural detailing that Santmyers would take to a further degree two years later at 2101 Connecticut Avenue.

Many years later, in 1976, with the urban renewal movement reaching Kalorama Triangle, the Mintwood Corporation, now the owner of the Mintwood Apartments at 1843 Mintwood Place, brought suit against six of its tenants who refused to move out so that the building could be converted to condominiums. But the D.C. Superior Court dismissed the suit, as the Mintwood Corporation had not issued valid eviction notices. Four tenants had signed consent agreements under undue influence and without the benefit of an attorney, and they were ruled invalid. The judge's decision stated that many of the tenants had a special need for lawyers. Some were too old and frightened or had limited use of English, spoke only Spanish or had limited education, and all were of low to moderate incomes. Previously, one hundred tenants from throughout the city had marched from the Mintwood apartments to the office of Columbia Management protesting against citywide evictions. After the judge's decision on the evictions, they held an all-day celebratory block party on Mintwood Place.

GEORGE TRUESDELL'S ADDITION TO WASHINGTON HEIGHTS

In 1887, when George Truesdell subdivided part of his property, creating the subdivision Truesdell's Addition to Washington Heights, an advertisement in the *Washington Post* promoted the concept of living along the future Connecticut Avenue (Ashmead Place) and its proximity to Woodley Lane:

> *Perhaps the best located property…in the city of Washington. Bounded as it is by Kalorama Avenue on the south, Twentieth Street on the west, and that most delightful of all suburban drives, Woodley Lane on the north, with Connecticut Avenue extended dividing the property in half, so that many of the lots lay along that popular thoroughfare, makes this subdivision at once exceedingly desirable for first-class residences.[47]*

But Truesdell's subdivision was far from ready for development. The land began to slope into the valley of Rock Creek at about Twentieth Street. In December 1887, Truesdell submitted a plan to the District commissioners to level the land between Kalorama Road and Connecticut Avenue Extended, using landfill removed from a current project widening Columbia Road. But the commissioners decided that the law should apply to city streets only and not include suburban "highways," which were still mostly privately owned. Truesdell did locate a source for landfill and filled in from Kalorama to Belmont Road, where the land now cuts off suddenly into Rock Creek.

Thomas J.D. Fuller House (2317 Ashmead Place)

The oldest extant house in Kalorama Triangle and the first to be built in Truesdell's subdivision was the Fuller house at 2317 Ashmead Place, designed by its owner, prominent architect Thomas J.D. Fuller, and built in 1893.

Fuller designed his house in the English Free Style that embodied characteristics of the Arts and Crafts movement, mixed with a free application of traditional architectural elements. Georgian period

The Thomas J.D. Fuller house at 2317 Ashmead Place. *Photo by the author.*

Thomas J.D. Fuller. *Courtesy Washingtoniana Room, Martin Luther King Library.*

architectural features dominate the first floor, with Flemish bond red brick, a doorway surmounted by a broken pediment and twelve-over-twelve paned windows. Drawing on the Arts and Crafts movement, the glass panel front door is accentuated with a tracery motif. The second floor contrasts the brick texture of the first floor with smooth stucco. The rounded bays contain multi-paned Palladian-style windows, and the gabled dormers in the roof are shingled in the Arts and Crafts tradition.

In 1892, Fuller examined the site for his new house located on Connecticut Avenue Extended (now Ashmead Place). At this time, there were no houses on the block. The street was paved only a distance down from Kalorama Road, with sidewalks and parking. The north part of the block was terraced, providing a sweeping view of Rock Creek. Unaware of existing lot divisions, Fuller selected the site based on its physical location. He then instructed his attorney to have the land surveyed and to obtain the deed from George Truesdell. Not knowing that he had actually bought the adjacent lot instead, Fuller then built his house on the lot he thought he had purchased. He enclosed the lot with a fence, hedges and terraces and planted trees and shrubs. Fuller remained unaware of the fact that he had built on the wrong lot until he complained to the health office of "the rank growth of weeds upon the adjoining lot" and was in turn informed that it was his own duty to remove the weeds, as the lot was his property.[48]

In 1912, former congressman Samuel H. McMillan brought suit against Fuller. McMillan claimed to be the rightful owner of the lot and wanted to recover it. He claimed to have purchased it in February 1910 and a year later discovered that there was a building on it. When he purchased the lot, he went to view it and saw Fuller's house but did not know that it was on the lot he had purchased. At the time, he was contemplating building an apartment building and considered Fuller's house to be an obstacle to this plans. Fuller offered to exchange lots with McMillan, who rejected the offer and took Fuller to court. Ultimately, the jury ruled in favor of Fuller, and he kept both the lot and his house.

Thomas Fuller probably wished that he had built his house on the actual lot he had purchased from Truesdell. Not aware of the allotted sizes and divisions of the lots on Ashmead, he had also overlooked a very large lot to the right, where in 1919 the Carthage apartment building would be built. The new building not only overpowered Fuller's house in mass but was flush to the side of his house, totally blocking the side's exposure. In spite of this, five generations of the Fullers continuously occupied the house until 1973. It was listed on the National Register of Historic Places in 1985.

By 1918, Fuller had acquired what was his original lot as well. He designed two three-story town houses (2319 and 2321 Ashmead Place) himself and contracted builder William A. Hill to have them built. Number 2319 Ashmead Place was purchased by Representative Hamilton Fish III, who lived there until the end of his political days in 1945.

Hamilton Fish III

Hamilton Stuyvesant Fish III served as a U.S. member of Congress from 1920 to 1945. At the outset of U.S. involvement in World War I, Fish was made a captain of the 369th U.S. Infantry Regiment, a unit composed of African American enlisted men that came to be famously known as the Harlem Hellfighters. The 369th spent 191 days on the front lines, which was the longest of any American regiment, and was also the first Allied regiment to reach the Rhine River. Fish—as well as his sister Janet, who served as a nurse near the front lines—was later inducted into the French Legion of Honor for his wartime service.

As a congressman, he was a strong anti-communist and an outspoken opponent of Franklin D. Roosevelt. Fish's political career ended when he lost the Republican general election in 1944. In 1921, Fish married Grace Chapin Rogers. Their son, Hamilton Fish IV, was a thirteen-term U.S. representative from New York from 1969 to 1995.

Hamilton Fish celebrated his 102nd birthday in 1990 and died a month later in January 1991. Throughout his life, Fish kept track of the men of the 369th U.S. Infantry Regiment. During his funeral at West Point, a group of veterans from the 369th arrived by bus from New York City. Upon

Representative Hamilton Fish III of New York lived at 2319 Ashmead Place during his nearly twenty-five years in Congress. During World War I, Fish was captain of the 369th U.S. Infantry Regiment, a unit composed of African American enlisted men that came to be famously known as the Harlem Hellfighters. *Courtesy Library of Congress, Prints and Photographs Division.*

being greeted by a family member and thanking them for being there for the service, one of the veterans said, "He [Fish] was always there when we needed him. We want to be here for him today."[49]

The Carthage (2301 Connecticut Avenue)

The Carthage at 2301 Connecticut Avenue, situated at the bend of Connecticut Avenue between Kalorama Road and Ashmead Place, was built in 1919 for renowned research chemist Dr. Artherton Seidell and was designed by the Bates Warren's architect, G. Neal Bell, and his partner, A.S. Rich.

Artherton Seidell was born in 1878 and came to Washington, D.C., in 1900. He was a pioneer in the areas of vitamin research and nutrition and was one of a team of scientists that discovered vitamins B-1 and B-2. After his retirement in 1936, he worked as consulting chemist with the Pasteur

The Carthage at
2301 Connecticut
Avenue. *HABS.*
*Courtesy Library of
Congress, Prints and
Photographs Division.*

Institute in Paris. For his work, he was inducted into the French Legion of
Honor and the Italian Order of the Crown. He was a strong proponent
of the use of microfilm for the management of scientific information and
was a founder of the American Documentation Institute (now the American
Society for Information Science). To promote the use of microfilm, Seidell
developed a simple and inexpensive microfilm reading device, known as the
"Seidell viewer," that was used in the 1940s and 1950s. Seidell lived at the
Carthage until his death in 1961.

The curved side of the Carthage along Ashmead Place echoes the curve
of the building's actual lot. Its beautifully maintained lawn, appreciated by
both neighbors and visitors alike, actually sits on a separate lot of land that
was reserved by the city when plans were being made to extend Connecticut
Avenue to Woodley Lane (now Belmont Road) through Ashmead Place in
the 1880s. It was later transferred to the National Park Service and is now
under the auspices of the Rock Creek Park.

The First Town Houses in Truesdell's Addition

The first town houses built in Truesdell's subdivision were a series of semi-
detached dwellings on Kalorama Road in 1897. The north side lots covering
2001–17 Kalorama Road and around the corner at 2308–10 Twentieth
Street were sold to real estate speculator C.J. Ubhoff. Working with

The house of architect Reginald Wyckliffe Geare at 2328 Twentieth Street. In addition to designing many homes in Kalorama Triangle, Geare also designed the Knickerbocker Theater. *Photo by the author.*

architect Edward Woltz, he constructed a series of paired, semi-detached, Romanesque Revival–style houses on speculation. Each building consisted of two units attached via a central party wall and sized to permit front, rear and side yards. This duplex design was later used by developer Harry Wardman along Columbia Road.

Probably the most prolific architect-builder team in Truesdell's Addition to Washington Heights was builder Ernest Walker and architect Reginald Wyckliffe Geare. Together, they constructed a total of twenty-four Mission Revival–style houses in 1913–14 in the 1900 block of Belmont Road, the 2300 block of Twentieth Street and Ashmead Place. Geare designed the last of these houses at 2328 Twentieth Street as his own residence. Geare's promising career as an architect was destroyed on the night of January 28, 1922, when the roof of the Knickerbocker Theater, which he designed in 1917, collapsed under the weight of heavy snow.

Ashmead Place: The Street with a View

Ashmead Place has been known by several names. When the street was first laid out, it was Connecticut Avenue Extended, and a short while thereafter, it became known as Old Connecticut Avenue. In 1907, it became Ashmead Place, named after Thomas J.D. Fuller's wife, Elizabeth Ashmead Schaeffer.

Perhaps no street was as much a showplace for real estate development in Kalorama Triangle as Ashmead Place, which was the subject of some questionable real estate promotions as well. Advertisements by real estate firms promoted Ashmead Place with its unobstructed views of "government park" and the new Million Dollar (Taft) Bridge. To start, Truesdell began selling lots on the south side of Ashmead Place that did, in fact, offer what was advertised.

In 1910, five lots on Ashmead Place (numbers 2341–49) were sold to real estate speculators Louis C. and Donie H. Ferrell, where they built five Mission Revival–style houses. Three years later, these houses were still on the market at an asking price of $12,500. One of the first buyers was Dr. Harvey W. Wiley, the first commissioner of the U.S. Food and Drug Administration, in 1913. That same year, construction began on three much more modest homes farther up the street at 2323–27 Ashmead Place. While designed by prominent architect William Allard, their modest scale was probably the result of a softer than expected real estate market. They were priced at $8,000.

In 1914, architect Reginald Wyckliffe Geare designed four Mission Revival–style houses at the foot of Ashmead Place and Twentieth Street.

Ashmead Place, circa 1914. *Courtesy Christopher and Elizabeth Naab.*

Dr. Harvey W. Willey, the first commissioner of the U.S. Food and Drug Administration, lived at 2345 Ashmead Place. *Courtesy Library of Congress, Prints and Photographs Division.*

The following year, five more Mission Revival–style homes were built on speculation on Ashmead Place by developer Ernest G. Walker and designed by Matthew G. Lepley. These houses, built five years later than 2341–49 Ashmead, boasted better amenities than the neighboring houses and were designed to sell at $21,500.

Then, in 1920, with all the lots on the south side of Ashmead sold, there was no incentive to hold back on developing the other side of the street. The Riviera Apartments at 2310 Ashmead Place (Kilpin House) was the first building on the north side of Ashmead Place behind the Woodward, on land many were led by developers and realtors to believe was a government-owned park.

In 1921, real estate developer C.H. Small & Co. acquired almost the entire north side of the street and, working with the architectural firm of Sonnemann & Justement, constructed nine two-story houses between 2312 and 2328 Ashmead Place. In 1922, Charles H. Davidson erected the Park Crest at 2308 Ashmead Place. With the north side of Ashmead now completely developed, what was once an unobstructed view of a government park and the Million Dollar Bridge for the original buyers had been totally blocked. But the new owners on the north side of Ashmead were not long to enjoy the former views of their neighbors across the street. In 1927, the houses on the north side were completely engulfed by the shadow of the Valley Vista apartment building.

The Valley Vista

The Valley Vista is one of the largest apartment buildings in Kalorama Triangle and the last one built in Truesdell's subdivision. It was built in 1927 and designed by Louis Justement, who specialized in large-scale housing projects and had worked with Garrett Sonnemann to build the row of houses on the north side of Ashmead five years earlier. The Valley Vista is noteworthy for its modern massing and an eclectic use of Art Deco elements, with a pair of sphinxes over the entrance on Ashmead Place, large Georgian Revival–style corner stones or quoins and Romanesque-style arches at the top of the bays facing Rock Creek Park. Unlike some of Kalorama Triangle's other large apartment buildings, the Valley Vista was built to accommodate Washington's burgeoning middle-class population with affordable modern conveniences, including sun rooms or balconies overlooking the park. With the completion of the Valley Vista, now only its residents had views of Rock Creek and the bridge.

The ground level of the Valley Vista on Ashmead Place was once home to the Valley Vista Pharmacy, which Harry Schwartz opened in 1936. Harry's son Ned, then owner, realizing in 2001 that both he and the pharmacy had reached the age of sixty-five, decided it was time that they both should retire. The pharmacy was converted into a condo unit.

PRETTY PROSPECT (WAGGAMAN'S SUBDIVISION)

Thomas Ennalls Waggaman, real estate broker and auctioneer, was born in Fairfax County, Virginia, in 1839. He studied at Georgetown University

Developer Thomas Ennalls Waggaman in his home art gallery on O Street in Georgetown. *In Slauson*, A History.

but was unable to complete his studies due to consumption. As with many young men at the time, he went west and made money in a freight company. Upon his return to Washington five years later, he went into the real estate business. He became interested in the development of the northwestern section of the city and acquired parts of Kalorama that had originally been part of the Pretty Prospect, Kalorama and Widow's Mite tracts of land bordering on Rock Creek to the east. He donated four squares of land through Woodley Park for the extension of Connecticut Avenue.

Situated on a steep slope toward Rock Creek that had been likened to the Dakota Badlands, much of the land was unimproved and unusable as it was. To correct the undevelopable landscape, Waggaman contracted H. Pierre Waggaman to erect a retaining wall to reclaim a portion of the property from the Rock Creek Valley. The wall was fifty feet high and ranged in thickness from eight feet at the base to two feet at the top. Waggaman leveled off an area of little wooded hills and filled in behind the wall to create a building plat. He planned on an extended Waterside Drive that would pass his development to the west. In 1892, drawing its name from the eighteenth-century tract of land on which it was partially located, Waggaman brought his new subdivision, Pretty Prospect—also known as Waggaman's subdivision—onto the market.

At the height of his prosperity, Waggaman was the biggest landlord in Washington, with properties in every residential neighborhood in the city and several thousand families as tenants. He acquired a significant art collection valued at almost $1 million, and for years it was customary for people who came to see Washington to also visit his private gallery at his home in Georgetown at 3300 O Street.

Waggaman's plans for his subdivision never fully materialized. The same year that the subdivision was brought on the market, the retaining wall collapsed. Fortunately, this occurred before the landfill behind it supported any buildings. Waggaman had it rebuilt. Even with the extension of the Rock Creek Railway just north of the property in 1891, Waggaman's subdivision did not begin to be developed until 1910 with Samuel Woodward's new apartment project, the Airy View.

Waggaman's life, including his subdivision, was fraught with tragedy. Most of the land he acquired bordering Rock Creek was unimproved, and the burden of carrying it in that condition was a great drain on his resources. For years, he looked forward to the development of his acres in Kalorama Triangle and the handsome returns on the capital that he had tied up in them, but his demise came before the significant rise in land values.

By 1904, Waggaman was bankrupt. He was declared the defendant in a suit in the District Supreme Court brought by the Second National Bank, the National Bank of Washington and the National Metropolitan Bank of Washington, all holders of Waggaman's promissory notes. This action was followed by a suit brought by the Columbia National Bank and others, which was then followed by the filing of a large number of smaller claims, upon which no security had been given.

In August 1905, Waggaman was indicted for embezzlement and arrested, with bond set for $3,000. He suffered a nervous breakdown and, after posting bail, was taken to a small farmhouse near Annapolis, where he died in 1906 of cancer. Through three marriages, he had seventeen children. His sons Clarke and Eugene, who were half brothers, became noted local architects and designed several houses in Kalorama Triangle.

Waggaman did not envision the mix of houses, town houses and apartments that was to be found in Kalorama Triangle's other subdivisions. The 1903 *Baist's Real Estate Atlas of Surveys of Washington* shows the entire west side of the subdivision fully broken into narrow house lots, on average only twenty feet wide. Multiple narrow lots tended to attract developers who built stretches of row houses on speculation, which in turn would attract working-class homebuyers. But, as with Ashmead Place, developers knew that they could attract wealthier clients if they offered views of the Connecticut Avenue Bridge and Rock Creek, and Samuel Woodward was not one to pass up an opportunity to offer rooms with views in Kalorama Triangle.

The Airy View

In 1910, the Airy View Apartment House Company of Alexandria was incorporated in Virginia by Samuel W. Woodward, president; builder John H. Nolan, vice-president; and B.W. Parker, secretary. That same year, Nolan combined three lots on the west side of Twentieth Street and, along with architect L.E. Simpson, built one of the larger buildings in Kalorama Triangle, the Airy View at 2415 Twentieth Street. The building remains unique in Kalorama Triangle, as it is the only one with a central bay pushed back from the street to create an enclosed courtyard.

Although appropriately named at the time, the building's view was not to last long. Taking advantage of the cheaper, narrow lots across the street, in 1913, developer Charles W. King Jr. and architect N.R. Grimm built a string of two-story Colonial Revival–style town houses that occupy the entire 2400 block of Twentieth Street between Allen Place and Calvert Street. Still, in 1916, an advertisement in the *Washington Post* claimed that the Airy View overlooked the Connecticut Avenue Bridge and Rock Creek Valley. King would finish his run on row houses with two more at 2402–4 Twentieth Street, designed by A.H Sonnemann, in 1917.

Clarke Waggaman

Fittingly, the first larger town houses built in Thomas Waggaman's subdivision were designed by his son Daniel Boone Clarke Waggaman in 1915 and built by Robert P. Hill. This was a set of four houses anchored at 2400 Twentieth Street and 2003–7 Belmont Road. Hill sold the house at 2400 Twentieth Street to Colonel Graham Fitch, a graduate of West Point and retired U.S. Army officer. The Fitches would tragically lose their son, Lieutenant Graham Newell Fitch, when the submarine he was on was rammed by a U.S. Coast Guard cutter and sank in 1927. The Fitches would continue to occupy the house until 1932, when Colonel Finch died at the age of seventy-two. Fitch's widow, Hermione King Fitch, then moved to the Kennedy-Warren apartments at 3133 Connecticut Avenue NW until her death in 1951.

Upon the insistence of his father, Clarke Waggaman studied law and graduated from Catholic University of America in June 1901. When Thomas Waggaman's career as a real estate broker ended so tragically,

Thomas Waggaman's son Clarke designed these houses at 2400 Twentieth Street and 2003–7 Belmont Road in 1915. *Photo by the author.*

Clarke started designing houses, although he had no formal training in architecture. Clarke's half brother Eugene, who was a trained architect, helped provide some of the needed technical assistance. In 1917, Clarke joined with architect George N. Ray and created the firm of Waggaman and Ray. That same year, Clarke Waggaman was elected to the American Institute of Architects. After a short but successful career, he died from the Spanish flu in 1919.

Allen Place

The houses on Allen Place were all built between 1919 and 1920 by builder C.H. Small and were designed by architect W.E. Howser. These two rows of houses reflect a combination of the Mission Revival and Arts and Crafts styles with red tile roofs, patterned brickwork and overhanging eaves with exposed rafters. When they were put on the market by Small in 1920, he advertised that these houses fronted on the Million Dollar Bridge and Rock Creek Park, as would the houses he would build on the north side of Ashmead Place a year later. As a sign of the changing times, these houses offered room for a garage as well.

Waterside Drive

By the early 1920s, several lots on Belmont Road and Waterside Drive, which still offered views of Rock Creek Park, had yet to be developed. These lots provided an opportunity for architects and builders to break with architectural tradition. Developer J.T. Hendrick would commission the new firm of Wardman & Waggaman (Harry Wardman and Clarke Waggaman's half brother Eugene) to build three town houses at 2021–25 Belmont in 1922.

While the Cliffbourne house may have been the first freestanding house in Kalorama Triangle, 2033 Waterside Drive, constructed in 1926 for William Lemon and designed by Claude Norton, was the last. Fittingly, the house represents a significant break in the architectural styles previously employed in Kalorama Triangle, adhering less to one specific style. Its asymmetrical design references medieval and Norman features, with a tower with a parapet and an unadorned arched door, a stucco exterior and a stone chimney.

While the Cliffbourne house was the first freestanding house built in Kalorama, 2033 Waterside Drive was the last in 1926. *Photo by the author.*

CLIFFBOURNE SUBDIVISION

In 1887, the Cliffbourne estate had been mapped out with tentative building lots and villa sites and was bought by Mrs. Effie Kline. Effie Kline probably had no intentions of developing the tract with actual streets, sidewalks and utilities herself but bought it as a short-term investment. In 1889, she was sued by developer Otis F. Presbrey for failing to deliver on a contract to sell Cliffbourne to him for $110,000, for which she had already received an advance payment of $5,000. She refused to sign the deed or refund the money. She may have learned in advance that the Rock Creek Railway was planning to extend through the property and that the financial gain of holding out for a better price was well worth the costs of a lawsuit. The case was ultimately dismissed.

Kline was born Effie Hinckley Ober in 1844 in Sedgwick, Maine. She decided to bring Gilbert and Sullivan's operetta *H.M.S. Pinafore* to the United States, specifically to stage a realistic or "ideal" performance of the operetta in November 1878. The performance took place on a ship in a lake in Boston's Oakland Park. In 1879, she organized the Boston Ideal Opera Company and served as its theatrical agent. Kline took the Boston Ideal Opera Company on the road, performing light operas all over the country. How Effie Kline ended up in Washington and the owner of Cliffbourne is a bit of a mystery.

In 1893, Effie Kline sold Cliffbourne to Francis G. Newlands for $185,000. In 1894, Newlands began laying Cincinnati Street (now Calvert) running along the Rock Creek Railway tracks, and in 1898, he brought the Cliffbourne subdivision onto the market. While it was the last subdivision created in Kalorama Triangle, it proved to be the most rapidly developed.

Calvert Street

No street in Kalorama Triangle experienced as rapid a development as did Calvert Street. Hoping to capitalize on the Rock Creek Railway streetcar stop and turn around (the "loop") just before the Calvert Street Bridge, speculators built almost all the town houses on the 1800 and 1900 blocks of Calvert and Biltmore Streets between the years 1900 and 1904. The firm of Meyers & Wunderly built more than thirty houses on Calvert and Biltmore Streets between the years 1904 and 1905 alone. These homes were bought by high-level civil servants, businessmen and retired military officers.

One of the four Arts and Crafts–style houses on the corner of Calvert Street and Cliffbourne Place designed by Waddy Butler Wood. *Photo by the author.*

Prominent Washington architects also joined the fray and designed and built houses on Calvert Street on speculation. Arthur Heaton, architect of the Altamont, designed two Gothic Revival–style houses at 1847 and 1849 Calvert Street. Waddy Wood built a block of four Arts and Crafts–style houses at the intersection of Cliffbourne and Calvert Streets (1902–6 Calvert and 2516 Cliffbourne) in 1900–1. Wood built the house at 1902 Calvert Street for his daughter Virginia, who was a locally renowned artist during her time.

In addition to residences in Calvert Street and Cliffbourne Place, Wood also designed the streetcar loop turnaround and waiting station on Calvert Street for the Capital Traction Company in 1899. Part of the building remains today on the site of the bus turnaround, but it has been significantly altered and lacks the large, hipped canopy roof that once covered an outside seating area.

The Cliffbourne (1915 Calvert Street)

The focus on individual upper-middle-class houses shifted in 1905 to apartments with the construction of the Cliffbourne apartment building at 1855 Calvert, designed by architect N.R Grimm, and the Sterling at 1915 Calvert Street, designed by Appleton P. Clark.

The Cliffbourne contained twenty-five modern housekeeping apartments of four, five and six rooms, each with a bath. At the time it was built, it was detached on every side and offered light and ventilation, as well as views overlooking Rock Creek Valley. Unlike other apartment buildings designed for the working class, building managers Lieberman and Hahn devised an innovative seasonal-style leasing system for the rental of their apartments. Hoping to capitalize on Washington's wealthier transient population, they sought to attract tenants in town for the congressional term and military officers in the process of transferring to posts outside the city.

In 1905, Thomas Dobyns, owner of the Cliffbourne flats at Eighteenth and Columbia and owner of 1957 Biltmore Street, filed a protest with the District commissioners complaining that Lieberman and Hahn had also named their building the Cliffbourne. He claimed that Cliffbourne had been the name of his flats since their construction and the new name would cause no end of confusion. The commissioners concluded that there was no regulation in the District for naming apartment buildings, and therefore, a man may give his apartment building "any old name."[50]

The Beacon (1801 Calvert Street)

Built by Joseph J. Moebs in 1910, the flatiron-shaped Beacon apartment building at 1801 Calvert Street was designed to be fireproof and featured a center light well to allow natural light into the apartments' inner rooms. It originally contained thirty-three housekeeping apartments with a restaurant

The Beacon at 1801 Calvert Street was built in 1910 as a fireproof building. In 1990, the damage from a fire burning out of control for over three hours took almost a year to repair. *Courtesy Library of Congress, Prints and Photographs Division.*

on the ground floor. The light well was filled in to create extra units when the building was converted to condominiums in 1985.

The Beacon was bought by Harry M. Crandall in 1920, owner of Crandall's Theaters and the Knickerbocker Theater at the corner of Eighteenth Street and Columbia Road. Crandall's objective was to remodel the building, making it one of the most attractive apartments in the city. After the Knickerbocker Theater disaster in 1922, Crandall sold the Beacon to Franklin Sanner's daughter Laura Sanner Post at a loss for $180,000.

In December 1990, a fire burning out of control for over three hours engulfed the top floor of the Beacon. Water cannons shooting millions of gallons onto the roof left the fireproof building uninhabitable. Firefighters were unable to access the fire, as it was trapped between the building's roof and a lower false roof. It took almost a year to reconstruct the condominium units, and its owners lost their homestead tax exemption in the process.

The Gotham: A Commune on Calvert Street

The site occupied by the town houses between 1945 and 1955 Calvert Street was once the Gotham Apartments. Built in 1911, this once elegant sixteen-unit apartment building became the scene of tenant resistance to urban renewal in the 1970s. The owners of the building, Jacob and Maurice Shapiro, initially bought the building in 1938 and planned to demolish it in the 1950s for an eight-story, six-wing apartment building. The plan failed, and in 1970, they tried again to construct a one-thousand-unit-plus apartment building overlooking the zoo at the eastern end of the Calvert Street Bridge. The building would have extended back onto part of the landfill that is now Walter Pierce Park.

Residents of the Gotham were given their eviction notices but failed to move out of the building. U.S. marshals were called in to physically remove the residents and their furnishings from the building. Residents of one apartment threw hot water, paint, bottles and bricks at the marshals and then set the apartment on fire. As soon as the marshals had left, the residents moved their furniture back into the building. Ultimately, the U.S. marshals were successful in carrying out the final evictions. But prior to the demolition of the building in 1971 for the construction of the present town houses, a mimeographed letter signed by "The White Rabbit" was widely distributed in the neighborhood that threatened to use guns, fire and dynamite if anyone approached the building. The tenants claimed no connection to the letter, and some admitted to placing a statement published in an underground newspaper accusing the police of fabricating the letter.[51]

Adams Mill Road

One of the bounding streets of Kalorama Triangle to the north is Adams Mill Road, which begins at the intersection of Columbia Road and Eighteenth Street. Its name comes from its history as the road that led to the plaster and gristmills on Rock Creek once owned by John Quincy Adams. The mills were probably built in the 1790s by Benjamin Stoddert, the first secretary of the navy, and were purchased by Adams in 1823 and remained in the Adams family until the 1870s. While no trace of the mills exist today, an early nineteenth-century house known today as Holt House, which served as the mill seat, still stands on what is now the grounds of the National Zoo.

Now known as the L'Aiglon Building, the original part of the building at 1808 Adams Mill Road was constructed in 1904 by prominent local builder and real estate magnate Franklin T. Sanner as his home. The original three-story brick house was set back from the street, with a mansard roof and gabled dormer windows on all four sides. Sanner chose for his architect the designer of the Wyoming apartment building, B. Stanley Simmons. Sanner lived at the house from 1904 until his death in 1916. The year before he died, he again worked with Simmons and built a three-story building with storefronts next door to his house at 1801 Columbia Road. The space has served as a drugstore and several restaurants and is now occupied by Starbucks.

The demand for commercial storefront space in the 1920s spread to Sanner's home itself. In 1923, the façade was removed and the current three-story curved building was wrapped around the front of the house. Much of the original red brick house behind the addition is still visible. The elegant Federal-style doorway with its glass fan and side lights, as well as the main staircase and stained-glass window on the landing, can still be seen through the glass entry doors at 1808 Adams Mill Road.

Biltmore Street

The 1800 block of Biltmore became home to several of Washington's nouveau riche. These self-made men turned to prominent architects to build homes that would serve as statements of their newly acquired wealth and

The home of Edward J. Stellwagen once stood at 1801 Biltmore Street. It is now the site of the Melwood apartment building at 1803 Biltmore. *Courtesy the Historical Society of Washington, D.C.*

social status. The first on the block was built for Edward J. Stellwagen at the corner of Columbia Road and Biltmore Street in 1899. Stellwagen was vice-president of the Rock Creek Railway Company and, along with his Biltmore Street neighbor, wealthy plumber Charles Thorn, was one of the incorporators of the Union Trust and Storage Company of the District of Columbia in 1890.

Stellwagen's house only stood for twenty-seven years. Changes in zoning allowing commercial development along the 1800 block of Columbia Road made the houses located there targets for demolition. In 1926, Harry Wardman, then owner of Wardman Construction Company, having had three of his own buildings along Columbia Road razed earlier for business development, would raze the Stellwagen house to build the mixed-use Melwood apartment building at 1803 Biltmore. In addition to being one of the largest apartment buildings in Kalorama Triangle, this eight-story building created space for additional storefronts on Columbia Road. Stores in the building have included the Grand Union Supermarket, CVS Pharmacy and Blockbuster Video. A&B Liquor has been in the building since 1941.

Just to the west of Stellwagen's house, along the north side of the 1800 block of Biltmore, were a number of large, freestanding homes built right

The Melwood apartment building was built by Harry Wardman in 1926. In addition to apartments, it also provided much-needed commercial space in Kalorama Triangle. *Courtesy of the Washingtoniana Room, Martin Luther King Library.*

after the turn of the twentieth century, only one of which remains today. These houses, including the former Vatican embassy, would later become the campus of a preparatory school for young men and are now the site of the Biltmore Mews town house complex.

William A. Gieseking (1807 Biltmore Street)

The next to build on the block was Riggs Bank employee William A. Gieseking. Gieseking built the once handsome Georgian Revival house at 1807 Biltmore Street in 1905. It was designed by C.A. Miller and built by John H. Nolan. Nolan followed precedents set by L. Norris's design of the Heyl house at 2009 Wyoming Avenue and Waddy Wood's for the home of Arthur Keith at 2210 Twentieth Street, with narrow street frontage and taking advantage of its broad sides for windows and side gardens. While the house still stands, its first-floor front porch has been removed and the main entrance moved to the ground floor. The numerous windows on each side, while not filled in, are now blocked by the neighboring buildings.

In 1907, Gieseking sold his house at 1807 Biltmore and bought the lot on the corner of Biltmore and Twentieth Streets with a view of the park for the site of his new house. In 1908, he moved to the new three-story house at 1960 Biltmore Street, which was also designed by architect C.A. Miller and built by John H. Nolan. As with most homes bordering the eastern edges of the developments, it provided a view of the new Connecticut Avenue Bridge and Rock Creek Park. In 1911, taking advantage of the present real estate boom, and again working with Miller and Nolan, Gieseking built the two three-story houses next door at 1952–54 Biltmore.

In 1920, Gieseking's career ended. He was sued by the American Security and Trust Company and by Edward F. Looker, executor of the estate of Thomas Hyde, for nonpayment on a $2,000 promissory note. He had already been sentenced to serve three and a half years in the penitentiary on charges of embezzlement. Gieseking died in 1928 at the age of sixty, living in a rented room up the street at 1922 Biltmore.

From Grand Homes to a Campus

The north side of the 1800 block of Biltmore Street, just to the west of Gieseking's house, was once the site of three other freestanding houses. Like the homes of Lawrence Sands and Samuel Shedd, they made an ideal site for an urban campus once they became too expensive to maintain as private residences.

In 1906, Monsignor Falconio, the Vatican's ambassador, broke ground for the Apostolic Delegation and a chapel at 1811 Biltmore. The building was constructed by Neuman & Smith of New York and Washington, which had built the Walsh residence at 2020 Massachusetts Avenue in 1903. Charles G. Thorn, a successful plumber, built his house at 1821 Biltmore Street, which was designed by Waddy Wood in 1909.

Samuel Pannill Ficklen, a general agent of the United States Mutual Accident Association, built his house on the corner of Cliffbourne at 1823 Biltmore Street in 1914. The Georgian-style house was designed by Clarke Waggaman and built by John H. Nolan. While neither Charles Thorn nor Samuel Ficklen actually had much to do with high society themselves, their debutante daughters would be highlighted on Washington's social pages for years.

Above: The Apostolic Delegation once stood at 1811 Biltmore Street. *Courtesy the Historical Society of Washington, D.C.*

Below: Clarke Waggaman drawing for the façade of the Ficklen house at 1823 Biltmore Street. *Courtesy Library of Congress, Prints and Photographs Division.*

Dr. Anita Newcomb McGee lived at 1901 Biltmore and was the founder of the Army Nursing Corps. *Courtesy National Library of Medicine, National Institutes of Health.*

The former elegant homes of Samuel Ficklen and Charles Thorn, as well as the Vatican Embassy, became the new location for the campus of the Columbia Preparatory School, which had been located at 1519 Rhode Island Avenue NW. The school was started in 1901 and offered a curriculum to prepare students planning to enter the U.S. Naval Academy in Annapolis, Maryland. One of its most noteworthy graduates was U.S. District Court judge John Sirica, who graduated from the school in 1921 and oversaw the Watergate trials. The Columbia Preparatory School closed its doors in 1971 due to dwindling student enrollment and revenues. It was razed for the construction of Kalorama Mews town houses at 1809–31 Biltmore in 1973.

Perhaps one of the most noteworthy residents of Biltmore Street was Dr. Anita Newcomb McGee. Her Colonial Revival–style house on the corner of Cliffbourne Place at 1901 Biltmore Street was built in 1901 by Alex Miller and designed by the firm of Speiden & Speiden. McGee had just retired from the post of acting assistant surgeon general in charge of the Army Nursing Corps, which she had organized. The house received national acclaim in a 1902 issue of the *Architect's and Builder's Journal* for its hot-water heating system.

Providing a break in the series of town houses, the elegant, freestanding, Georgian Revival–style house at 1957 Biltmore was built in 1910 for pharmacy owner and landlord Thomas A. Dobyns. Dobyns became wealthy by launching a chain of pharmacies, one of which he opened at Eighteenth and Columbia, where his Cliffbourne Flats apartment building was also located. The house was designed by Appleton P. Clark and, like so many houses on Biltmore Street, was built by John Nolan.

Cliffbourne Place

The one-block Cliffbourne Place is the only street that runs between Calvert and Biltmore Streets. It was created to provide street access to the Cliffbourne estate, which was still standing when Newlands created his subdivision in 1898. The street has had its share of name changes. When it had just been laid, it was named Twentieth Street. In 1899, it was renamed Nineteenth Street at the request of Anita Newcomb McGee. In 1905, the name was changed to its current name, Cliffbourne Place, after the former estate. That year, Baltimore Street was renamed Biltmore and Cincinnati was renamed Calvert Street.

The first houses to be built on Cliffbourne Place were a pair of attached row houses at 2504–6 designed by Hornblower & Marshall in 1899. Hornblower & Marshall were known for their expertise in the grander Beaux-Arts style, embodied in their 1906 design of the Lothrop mansion. These two early houses are a study in simplicity, with minimal detailing, providing a break from the Georgian Revival style that was sweeping the neighborhood at the time.

The "Painted Ladies" of Cliffbourne Place. *Photo by the author.*

The house at 2504 Cliffbourne was built for journalist Robert Lincoln O'Brien, and 2506 Cliffbourne was built for Flora McDonald Thompson. In 1905, O'Brien wrote to the District commissioners commending them on their recent action in renaming the block and was especially pleased with the correct spelling of Cliffbourne.[52] Mrs. Thompson made the mistake of renting her house to Representative Wilfred W. Lukfin of Massachusetts in 1919. She ended up filing suit against Lukfin to recover damages he caused to her furniture.

In 1900, developer R.W. Walker and Frederick B. Pyle built a row of Arts and Crafts houses with large eaves overhanging decorative brickwork on the third floor across the corner from where Waddy Wood designed his the same year. Today, the buildings stand out with their bright and contrasting colors and are Kalorama Triangle's version of San Francisco's "Painted Ladies."

Calvert Street's Own Commercial District

While Eighteenth Street and Columbia Road still serve as the commercial district for Kalorama Triangle, the lower part of the 1900 block of Calvert was once also a small commercial district unto itself. It was an ideal location at the streetcar turnaround where commuters could pick up groceries and sundry items on their way home after disembarking from the streetcar.

The Black and White taxicab company maintained a taxi stop at the loop for years.

The ground floor of the house at 1954 Calvert Street, built in 1904, was originally the location of Post Office State No. 37 until it was transferred to Eighteenth and U Streets in 1914. That year, it became Loop Pharmacy, taking its name from the streetcar turnaround immediately across the street. The Loop Pharmacy survived until 1939, when an attempt was made to convert it into a restaurant. By 1948, it had become home to Walter Honeycutt's Honeycutt Upholsterers. The business proved to be successful, and by 1967, Honeycutt had opened two more stores at Bailey's Crossroads on Leesburg Pike in Virginia and in Rockville, Maryland. The Honeycutt shop remained open on Calvert Street until 1977.

About 1914, 1963 Calvert Street was a drugstore owned by James Montgomery Beall. In 1918, six of Beall's clerks were in active service in World War I. That year, one of Beall's employees and a boarder, twenty-seven-year-old James A. Clayton, was killed in the fighting of Chateau Thierry, France, earning the drugstore its first gold star on its service flag. Beall eventually sold the store to the Sanitary Grocery Chain, which had been acquiring small grocers in Washington. The Sanitary Grocery Chain was bought by Safeway in 1928.

The store had its share of misfortune. In 1940, two gunmen entered the store at a busy hour early in the evening and ordered everyone, including a dozen customers, into a back room, leaving only clerk Harwood Pointer in the front. While Pointer was emptying the cash register, Mrs. Yetta Katzman, a resident of 1937 Biltmore Street, entered the store and was told by the robbers to join the others in the back. But Mrs. Katzman had "trouble with her English" and did not understand the demand. After hesitating for a moment, she asked for the manager, at which point she was struck on the head by one of the robbers. She pulled through, although she was reported to be suffering of nervous shock later at her home. By 1958, the building had become home to Peel Cleaning Service, and it is now Rosa's Dry Cleaners.

Mama Ayesha's Calvert Café

The building that now is home to Mama Ayesha's Restaurant at 1967 Calvert Street began as Malby's Drug Company and ice cream parlor about 1907. By 1926, the store had become the Calvert Street Delicatessen. The establishment offered a bit more than just food. In 1931, police confiscated nine illegal slot machines from cigar stores, barbershops, groceries and

Mama Ayesha and Helen Thomas in their bright red outfits. *Courtesy of Mama Ayesha's Restaurant.*

other public gathering places. Two slot machines were confiscated from the Calvert Street Delicatessen.

In 1950, it became the site of the Calvert Café, a name that it still retains in part today. Mama Ayesha opened her café there in 1960. Perhaps no one knew Mama Ayesha or the history of the restaurant better than journalist and former White House correspondent Helen Thomas. In 1993, after Mama Ayesha had passed away, Thomas told the *Washington Post*:

> *Adams-Morgan was pretty seedy…highly transient, with a lot of boardinghouses, but Mama didn't care. If your money was good you were welcome. She couldn't read or write, but she sure knew what the figures on the bottom line said. She was a remarkable woman…entirely self-reliant. I don't think she ever asked anything of anyone.*
>
> *As I remember, she had been cussing the king. With help from some generals she got to Damascus, and ended up in Washington as a cook in the Syrian Embassy…The food was terrific and Mama was never one to hide her light under a bushel. She was out there taking bows.[53]*

In the early 1970s, Mama's cousin Joseph Howar's socialite wife introduced Henry Kissinger and other Nixon figures to Mama Ayesha's cooking. The Calvert Café became a "watering hole for the beautiful people."[54]

Mama Ayesha lived to be 103 years old, and her family continues to run the business. Until she died, she kept a watchful eye on the restaurant from her usual spot in the back booth and kept track of all the evening receipts. In her autobiography *Front Row at the White House: My life and Times*, Helen Thomas wrote of Mama Ayesha: "I know I'll never forget her. I can't. On the right-hand wall above my table is a picture of the two of us, both dressed in bright red outfits."[55]

GENERAL GEORGE McCLELLAN'S STATUE

Gateway to the Neighborhood

The most prominent landmark anchor to Kalorama Triangle is the equestrian statue of General George McClellan that stands on the triangular park at the corner of Connecticut Avenue and Columbia Road. While its serves as a proud gateway to Kalorama Triangle, its final location was actually a last-minute decision.

In 1901, Congress appropriated $50,000 for the preparation of a site and the erection of a pedestal for a statue of Major General George McClellan, one of the many generals selected and then fired by Abraham Lincoln to lead the Union army during the Civil War. The selection of the site would be supervised by the McClellan Statue Commission, which included then secretary of war William Howard Taft. The commission also created an advisory committee to provide recommendations. It was initially decided that Sheridan Circle would be the site for the proposed McClellan statue, and Mrs. McClellan and his son, Representative George B. McClellan, wrote to the McClellan monument committee of the Society of the Army of the Potomac approving the location.

The statue commission sponsored a competition, inviting artists who were U.S. citizens to submit models by May 1, 1902. The commission would select four models it considered to be the best. The committee selected models submitted by Austin Hays, Waldo Story, Charles Niehaus and Attil Piccirilli. The advisory committee recommended the sculpture by Niehaus with some

The statue of General McClellan serves as the gateway to Kalorama Triangle. *Courtesy Library of Congress, Prints and Photographs Division.*

alterations, but its recommendation was rejected by the commission. The commission then invited sculptor Frederick MacMonnies to make the model for the statue for a set fee. By this time, the Sheridan Statue Commission had selected the site of what is now Sheridan Circle for the location of the statue of General Philip Sheridan.

In 1904, Frederick MacMonnies, whose bronze shop was located in Paris, accepted the offer of the commission to design and make the statue of McClellan, which by then was to be erected in the public reservation at the intersection of Connecticut Avenue and N Streets. MacMonnies's initial design had to be modified, as it required more money than was available. The modified design was approved by Mrs. McClellan and McClellan's lifelong friend General Warren.

The selection of MacMonnies to provide the statue caused a protest by domestic sculpture makers, who complained of discrimination, as some sculptors doing work for the government had their bronze-casting and marble cutting done abroad, with the finished product admitted duty-free as government property. This may well have been the first case of outsourcing experienced in Kalorama Triangle

On January 19, 1906, William Howard Taft, president of the McClellan Statue Commission, announced that the statue would be erected at the intersection of Columbia Road and Connecticut Avenue. The commission decided that the new site was more "satisfactory and imposing" than the one at Connecticut Avenue and N Streets. Taft wrote to the president of the Washington Heights Citizens Association (now the Kalorama Citizens Association) informing him that if Congress were to authorize the purchase of the land from George Truesdell, the statue commission would gladly move the statue to the location, provided that the Washington Heights Citizens Association pay for the expense of moving the statue.

The unveiling of the statue was to coincide with the thirty-seventh annual reunion of the Society of the Army of the Potomac on October 18, 1906, with addresses by President Roosevelt and others. The unveiling ceremony, as well as the society's reunion, was delayed due to a fire that destroyed MacMonnies's polishing works, preventing him from completing the pedestal. A new date was set for May 15 the following year. The unveiling of the statue actually occurred on May 2, 1907, and fortunately, President Theodore Roosevelt was still available to make the opening address. The statue is a D.C. historic landmark.

A CLASS APART

Connecticut Avenue Apartment Buildings

T hree large and distinctive apartment buildings border the east side of Connecticut Avenue on the curve before the Taft Bridge, two of which are generally only known by their street addresses. Unlike earlier apartment buildings in Kalorama Triangle, these buildings were conceived to be part of the new Connecticut Avenue corridor and are not as germane to the development of Kalorama Triangle as are its other apartment buildings. In fact, two of these buildings—2029 and 2101—share the same 20008 zip code as the Sheridan-Kalorama neighborhood, as the original subdivisions on which they were built lay mainly on the other side of Connecticut Avenue.

THE WOODWARD (2311 CONNECTICUT AVENUE)

The Woodward at 2311 Connecticut Avenue was built by Samuel Woodward and was the first apartment building constructed along the Kalorama Triangle side of Connecticut Avenue. Woodward, in addition to being a retail magnate, was one of Washington's noted builders. Woodward partnered with architect Frederick Pyle, who had designed so many town houses along Calvert and Biltmore Streets, to build eleven town houses on Leroy Place and Bancroft Place in 1907. Woodward had also built four modest apartment buildings in 1908 and 1912.

After incorporating the Woodley apartment building in 1903 and building four apartment buildings on his own, Woodward decided to build another

The Woodward apartment building located at 2311 Connecticut Avenue was built as an investment by Samuel Woodward in 1909. *Courtesy of the Washingtoniana Room, Martin Luther King Library.*

apartment building as a personal investment. In 1909, he selected a location not far from his house, along the curve where Connecticut Avenue connects to the Taft Bridge, to build his namesake apartment building.

He enlisted the architectural firm of Harding & Upman and, in 1909, started construction of a seven-story Mission Revival–style apartment house of brick and iron. When it was ready for occupancy in October 1910, it offered a total of forty-five rental apartments. Three apartments located over the building's entrance were duplex units, with a dining room, kitchen, pantry, parlor and library on the first level and three bedrooms and a bath on the second. The building offered many amenities that Truesdell would incorporate into the Altamont two years later. The Woodward had a roof garden, a summer pavilion and, like the Mendota, a doctor's office on the ground floor. The basement contained a party room, a billiard room and a barbershop.

The Woodward was bought in 1922 by Alonzo O. Bliss Properties Trust, which also bought the Little property from Christian Heurich in 1926. Arthur Bliss, Alonzo's son and owner of the company, took up residence in the Woodward and lived there until his death in 1953. The building was sold in 1968 to the Landmark Companies. In 1973, the Woodward would be converted into a condominium. It is a designated D.C. historic landmark.

BATES WARREN (2029 CONNECTICUT AVENUE)

Constructed in 1915, the Renaissance-inspired Bates Warren at 2029 Connecticut Avenue was built by developer Bates Warren and designed by architects Ernest C. Hunter and G. Neal Bell. Hunter and Bell also designed apartments in Washington Heights, including the Netherlands at 1860 Columbia Road (1909) and the Norwood at 1868 Columbia Road (1916). Bell would later partner with architect A.S. Rich to design the Carthage at 2301 Connecticut Avenue (1919).

The Bates Warren at 2029 Connecticut Avenue. *Photo by the author.*

Number 2029 Connecticut Avenue was built on the highest and most visible ground in Kalorama Triangle and on the same lot that Samuel Woodward had earlier chosen for his mansion in 1886. The building made extensive use of ivory-colored terra cotta facing on the first two floors, the top floor and roof cornice and on a highly ornate porch facing Connecticut Avenue. The architects were sensitive to design the building's massing so as not to dominate the Wood-Deming houses next door (or at least from behind). Unlike the Woodward, Mendota and Altamont buildings, the Bates Warren did not offer such amenities as barbershops or doctors' offices. Instead, the ground floor contained parlors for both men and women with restrooms where guests could prepare before their visits. The larger apartments that face Connecticut Avenue on the upper floors are 5,400 square feet in size.

When it opened as a rental in 1916, the ground floor consisted of four apartments and three per floor above, totaling only twenty-two units. In 1977, the building was purchased by Conrad Cafritz and converted into condominiums. The two parlors off the lobby were converted into efficiencies, and at the rear of the building, a two-level parking structure was added.

Some notable past occupants of 2029 Connecticut have included Joseph Gurney Cannon (fortieth Speaker of the House), Supreme Court justice William O. Douglas, singer Lena Horne, George McGovern, General John Pershing and former president and Supreme Court justice William Howard Taft when he was serving as secretary of war and was on the General McClellan Statue Commission.

2101 CONNECTICUT AVENUE

The last grand apartment building constructed in Kalorama Triangle, 2101 Connecticut Avenue, was built in 1927 by developer Harry M. Bralove and designed by Joseph Abel and George T. Santmyers. Only two years earlier, Bralove and Santmyers had built the apartment building at 1875 Mintwood Place, where they employed an eclectic architectural style with a Gothic theme that they would emphasize on this building as well.

The building is eight stories tall, consisting of three bays or wings, originally with sixty-four three-bedroom apartments, with one apartment per wing. Apartment sizes range from 2,600 to 3,200 square feet. Santmyers, following the examples set by the Woodward and the Altamont, planned the rooftop space for use as well, with two pavilions with Byzantine-style spiral columns. Bralove also built a 3,000-square-foot private deck on the

Number 2101 Connecticut Avenue. *HABS. Courtesy Library of Congress, Prints and Photographs Division.*

southwest corner over an apartment for one of his partners.[56] Perhaps the most notable features of its rooftop are the sixteen five-foot-high horned grinning demons holding balls over their heads, ready to toss at those who look up at them.

A two-level parking structure was added behind the building on the former site of the Eliza Barker house at 2011 Wyoming Avenue in 1954. The building was converted to a co-op in 1976.

THE KNICKERBOCKER THEATER
DISASTER OF 1922

The Knickerbocker Theater once stood on the southeast corner of Eighteenth Street and Columbia Road. It was built in 1917 for the Knickerbocker Theater Company, owned by Harry Crandall, who would also purchase the Beacon apartment building on Calvert Street in 1920. The Knickerbocker Theater was designed by architect Reginald Wyckliffe Geare, who, after his marriage in 1915, built a house for himself at 2328 Twentieth Street just a few blocks from the theater. When it was completed, the Knickerbocker Theater was the largest theater of its kind in Washington, D.C. In addition to serving as a movie theater, it also served as a concert and lecture hall, with ballrooms, luxurious parlors and lounges.

On January 27, 1922, Washington experienced its largest snowstorm on record. By the next morning, the total snowfall had reached eighteen inches, and when the storm tapered off the next morning, the official total was twenty-eight inches. Temperatures stayed in the low to mid-twenties during most of the storm.

On the evening of January 28, 1922, seeking a respite from the cold and snow, local residents flocked to the Knickerbocker to see the 1921 silent movie *Get-Rich-Quick Wallingford*. The roof of the Knickerbocker was flat, which, along with low temperatures during the storm, allowed the snow to accumulate on the roof throughout the storm. During the intermission of the movie, the weight of the snow split the roof down the middle, bringing down the balcony as well as a portion of an exterior brick wall, burying dozens of people. People with lanterns frantically attempted to

The Knickerbocker Theater after its roof collapsed on moviegoers on January 28, 1922, killing 98 people and injuring 133 more. *Courtesy Library of Congress, Prints and Photographs Division.*

rescue victims of the disaster. By midnight, 200 rescue workers were on the scene, and that number increased to more than 600 by 2:30 a.m. Nearby residents, including the theater's architect, Reginald Geare, helped pull bodies from the debris and feed the rescuers, also supplying them with hot drinks. Geare's knowledge of the building's design was invaluable in the rescue work. The Christian Science Church on Columbia Road became a temporary morgue. In all, 98 people were killed and 133 injured, many of whom were residents of Kalorama Triangle. This disaster still ranks as one of the worst in Washington, D.C. history, and the storm is still known as the Knickerbocker Storm.

In 1922, Reginald Geare, along with four other men, was indicted by a grand jury for manslaughter. Geare was charged with failing to draw the plans and designs of the theater in a skillful manner and failing to exercise general direction and supervision of work on the building while it was being constructed. Although none of the five men was convicted, Geare's career as an architect was destroyed by the disaster. Although he fought to reestablish his career, he could not recover from the blow and committed suicide in

1927 by turning on the gas in an attic room at his home at 3047 Porter Street. Harry Crandall committed suicide in 1937 after he lost his comeback project in Cleveland Park that had ultimately opened as Warner Brothers' new Uptown Theater the year before.

The site of the Knickerbocker Theater is now the location of SunTrust Bank. The building, in the shape of a movie theater, stands as a reminder of the Knickerbocker disaster.

URBAN RENEWAL

Kalorama Triangle Defines Itself

The name Kalorama Triangle did not begin to be used until the early 1960s during efforts to separate itself from other neighborhoods that were targets for urban renewal programs. Kalorama Triangle's unique sense of its history and identity, which helped preserve its basic character through urban decline, led it to distinguish itself from its neighbors and ultimately protect it from the potentially destructive urban renewal process that was going on around it.

By the beginning of the 1960s, Kalorama Triangle and its surrounds had reached middle age and were becoming run-down. The area experienced the effects of the Great Depression, World War II and the resulting housing crunch in the capital and the flight of the urban middle class to the suburbs. A 1960 study by the National Capital Planning Commission found that 24 percent of the buildings in the area were substandard and an additional 23 percent required major repairs—nearly half the buildings.

In 1960, a two-year federally assisted restoration project in the 243-acre Adams Morgan neighborhood was introduced. The chief aims of the project were to keep out rooming houses, tenements and tourist homes and to redevelop the commercial area located around Eighteenth and Columbia Roads. Project focus areas were Area A: Kalorama Triangle; Area B: Florida Avenue, Columbia Road and Eighteenth Street (now Washington Heights); and Area C: Florida Avenue and Eighteenth Street to Columbia Road and west to Sixteenth Street. The plan was championed by twenty-six neighborhood groups that formed the Citizens Planning Committee. The committee was led by Donald D. Gartenhaus, then owner of Gartenhaus Furs, which was located on the northwest corner of Columbia and Adams Mill Roads.

Four area citizens' organizations—the Kalorama Citizens Association, the Kalorama Triangle Restoration Society, the Ashmead Place Association and the Mintwood Place Improvement Association—objected to including Kalorama Triangle within the project boundaries. Small business owners were against the plan, as it would force them to move out of the area. Many were concerned that the project would be a repeat of the bulldozer approach taken in a similar renewal project in the southwest quadrant of the city.

On June 16, 1960, the Kalorama Citizens Association voted to oppose urban renewal in Kalorama Triangle. It asserted that the mostly single-family homes and luxury apartment buildings in Kalorama Triangle had been maintained. It did concede that one edge of the Triangle, specifically a row of rooming houses along Columbia Road, could use some renewal. District commissioners still went ahead and designated the entire Adams Morgan neighborhood as an urban renewal area, but the boundaries had yet to be worked out. Commissioners ultimately agreed that redevelopment efforts in the "so-called Kalorama triangle,"[57] falling between Columbia Road and Rock Creek Park, should be confined to conservation and rehabilitation.

In 1961, battle lines were being drawn over where the plan should be applied. Some groups were concerned about architecture and others about providing housing at rents that poor people could afford. Kalorama Triangle organizations still fought to exclude Area A from the plan. Hundreds of meetings were held.

By 1962, a change in the economic environment in the area helped relieve some of the pressure on Kalorama Triangle. News of the building of the Hilton Hotel on Connecticut Avenue started to drive up real estate prices. That same year, the Woodley apartment building on Columbia Road was renovated, tripling its value. The Rock Creek Hotel also opened at 2401 Twentieth Street with fifty-two rooms, completing a building project that included four affordable apartment buildings totaling 120 rentals and one hundred parking spaces.

By 1963, a final plan still had not been approved. There was disagreement over the forced relocation of small businesses, omission of neighborhoods where homes were in generally good condition—specifically Kalorama Triangle—and a provision that would allow the acquisition and conversion of scattered dwellings in public housing units, which proved to be the least popular feature of the plan. Kalorama Triangle felt that restoration would be enough.

Kalorama's residents became tired of waiting and took on the betterment of the neighborhood themselves to show that they did not need a federally funded renewal program. A building boom in 1964 and 1965 helped to remake, not revolutionize, Kalorama Triangle. It started to experience a residential rebirth through privately financed restorations and rehabilitations. Influenced by the work of the Kalorama Triangle Restoration Society, many homeowners took on the task of rehabilitating or restoring their homes. Sometimes not in the best interest of historic preservation, they began ripping off old, crumbling porches, painting brick façades, replacing windows and knocking out windows to create new doorways. Others began buying up tenement houses and converting them back into the grand, single-family homes they once were.

Kalorama Triangle's restoration efforts attracted two young developers who wanted to break into the building business in Kalorama Triangle. In 1965, twenty-five-year-old Thomas Nordlinger and twenty-eight-year-old Robert Berger built an eight-unit, three-story apartment building at 2001–5 Allen Place, siding with their office at 2428 Twentieth Street. They believed that their modern interpretation of the Georgian Revival style fit well with its turn-of-the-century neighbors.

Confidence in the real estate appeal of Kalorama Triangle's original houses continued to grow. In 1966, realtor Norman Bernstein bought up the row of seven town houses between 1961 and 1979 Biltmore Street that had been built on speculation in 1905 and had turned into rooming houses. His plan was to raze them and erect a high-rise apartment building on the site. But increased financing and construction costs caused him to drop his plan. He decided not to put the run-down houses back on the market, as that would have an adverse impact on neighboring property values and impair the general trend toward restoration in Kalorama Triangle. Instead, he completely renovated four of them and only restored the exteriors of the other three in order to sell those for less.

The demographics of the area were changing rapidly. Adams Morgan may have been integrated statistically, but it was not so geographically. By 1965, the population estimate was 23,000, of whom 11,100 were white, most of whom lived in Kalorama Triangle. In 1967, *Washington Post* writers Jim Hoagland and Richard Severo would describe how Kalorama Triangle had distinguished itself: "Residents in the Triangle are concerned with restoration, elegance, and the perpetuation of the good life as it exists in well-kept Washington town houses. Most residents of the Triangle readily identify with it—but not with the area to the east of it, which contains housing as undistinguished as the Triangle is distinguished."

The division between the east and west side of Columbia Road that became a dividing line with urban renewal in the 1960s left its mark. In 1987, the Kalorama Citizens Association assisted with the National Register of Historic Places nomination of Kalorama Triangle as a distinct nationally recognized historic district. Its boundary on the east was Columbia Road, omitting the area between Columbia Road and Eighteenth Street.

It is historically impossible to differentiate the histories of the east and west sides of Columbia Road, as each was part of the same original tracts of land belonging to Anthony Holmead and Robert Peter, and together they composed William Thornton's horse farm and John Little's estate. They developed at the same time, with many of the same architects and builders. Their residents could not be distinguished based on their socioeconomic situations, and famous persons lived on both sides of Columbia Road. The only major distinguishing fact is that Kalorama Triangle was home to several larger, freestanding homes. In 2006, the area between Columbia Road and Eighteenth Streets became its own historic district, taking the name of Corcoran's first subdivision, Washington Heights.

Into the 1990s, Kalorama was still attracting builders. In 1996, suburban builders Kettler Brothers Inc., best known for creating Montgomery Village in Maryland, built Kalorama Place, a 123-condominium town house complex in the center of Kalorama Triangle, and created Kalorama Triangle's newest street, Kalorama Place. Sensitive to Kalorama's proud architectural history, the complex was designed to echo the early nineteenth-century architectural themes of the surrounding row houses. It took the place of the Rock Creek Hotel, a relic of urban renewal. Replacing the hotel with condominiums was a final step in the neighborhood's return from a somewhat run-down area by the 1960s to the well-maintained, residential showplace that it had been.

Today's residents of Kalorama Triangle inherit a rich legacy, which hopefully this book has helped illuminate. The ambitions and energies of its builders created a diverse and bucolic urban village that reflects the variety of their visions. It is a place that occupies a special location on a pleasant hill bordering the northwestern urban core of the nation's capital. That special geography and the inherited urban landscape are enduring features of Kalorama Triangle. The stewardship of Kalorama Triangle is the privilege of both its current and future residents.

NOTES

The Origins of Kalorama Triangle

1. Proctor, "Indian Lore," 12–14.

The First Proprietors

2. Skordas, Brewer and Trader, *Early Settlers of Maryland*, 281.
3. Maryland Land Office Records, Liber 1 (1634–1655).
4. Peden, *Colonial Maryland Soldiers*, 215.
5. Baldwin and Henry, *Maryland Calendar of Wills*, 17.
6. Maryland Calendar of Wills, 1–13.
7. Horn, *Adapting to a New World*, 358–59.
8. Maryland Land Office Records, Liber 10, Folio 28.
9. Maryland Calendar of Wills, Liber 2, Folio 282.
10. Prince George's Land Records, Folio 320.
11. Prince George's County Wills, Liber 14, Folio 389.
12. McNeil, "Rock Creek Hundred," 37.
13. Prince George's County Wills, Liber 14, Folio 389.
14. Prince George's Land Records 1717–1726. Liber F, Folio 14/541.
15. "Poor Thomas" is a reference that has been used by Fletchall family genealogists.
16. Many believe that Rock Hill was the original name of the Kalorama estate. Anthony Holmead's daughter, Loveday Buchannan, inherited

Anthony Holmead's second house and lived there with her husband, Thomas Pairo. Pairo referred to the house as Rock Hill. Their daughter Sophia Kall inherited the house, and her funeral in 1894 was held at her late residence, Rock Hill.

KALORAMA TRIANGLE IN THE NINETEENTH CENTURY

17. Emery, "Mount Pleasant and Meridian Hill," 195.
18. D.C. Recorder of Deeds, Land Records Liber W. B., Folio 40.
19. D.C. Recorder of Deeds, Land Records "Richard Smith Trustee & George Bomford to Charles H. James." Recorded September 19, 1845.
20. D.C. Recorder of Deeds, Land Records. Liber W.B. 129, Folio 110.
21. D.C. Recorder of Deeds, Land Records Liber W.B. 129, Folio 119.
22. Mitchell, 174.
23. Thornton failed to record the original deeds of 1815 and 1817, probably in fear that his debts would be attached as liens on the titles. In 1822, new bonds of conveyance were drawn up with George Bomford as the trustee. Land in Thomas Peters's 1815 deed to Thornton is described in Liber W.B. 6, Folio 187, and in John Holmead's 1817 deed to Thornton in Liber W.B. 6, Folio 184.
24. Proctor, "Christian Hines," 37.
25. Proctor, "Beautiful Temple Heights."
26. Proctor, "Christian Hines," 39–40.
27. Provine, *Compensated Emancipation*.
28. Ibid.
29. *Washington Evening Star*, June 17, 1861.
30. Garrison, *John Shaw Billings*, 22.
31. Dammann and Bottet, "Images of Civil War Medicine," 122.
32. Ibid.
33. Billings, "Medical Reminiscences," 115–21.
34. Ibid.
35. D.C. Recorder of Deeds, Land Records, Liber 614, Folio 110–11.

CROSSING ROCK CREEK

36. *Washington Post*, "The District in Congress," February 28, 1888, 5.
37. *Streetcar and Bus Resources of Washington, D.C.*

38. *Washington Post*, "Rock Creek Railway: A Bill to Change the Route Discussed in the Senate," May 11, 1890, 2.

FROM COUNTRY ESTATES TO SUBURBIA

39. *Washington Post*, "Mr. Truesdell's New Subdivision," June 2, 1891, 1.
40. *Washington Post*, "Growth of the City Moves Steadily in the Northwestern Direction," April 1, 1906, R8. This was probably meant as a reference to Lawrence Sands. F.P.B. Sands actually lived at 1222 Connecticut Avenue.

KALORAMA TRIANGLE'S ORIGINAL SUBDIVISIONS

41. *Washington Post*, "Famous Washington Home Bought by Wife of White House Secretary," November 14, 1920; *Washington Post*, October 18, 1905.
42. *Washington Post*, "Extension of Twentieth Street," May 20, 1896.
43. *Washington Post*, "Sees No Money in Science." January 2, 1915.
44. "Declaration of Principles." International New Thought Alliance.
45. *Washington Post*, "Resurrection Cult Reports 'Progress,'" October 28, 1936.
46. *Washington Post*, "Mr. Childress Fetes Stag Group 'At Sea,'" August 4, 1929, S6.
47. *Washington Post*, "Mr. Truesdell's New Subdivision," June 2, 1891, 1.
48. Washington Law Reporter, Vol. 42.
49. Author's personal communication with the Fish family.
50. *Washington Post*, "No Copyright on Names," July 26, 1905, 12.
51. Paul Hodge, "Threat Halts Demolition of NW Building," *Washington Post*, December 10, 1970, C1.
52. *Washington Post*, October 18, 1905.
53. Ken Ringle and Megan Rosenfeld, "Mama Ayesha and a Menu Full of Memories." *Washington Post*, June 4, 1993, C1.
54. Ibid.
55. Thomas, *Front Row at the White House*, 64.

A Class Apart

56. Goode, *Best Addresses*, 226.

Urban Renewal

57. *Washington Post*, "Commissioners Vote Urban Renewal for Adams-Morgan Neighborhood," August 13, 1960.

BIBLIOGRAPHY

Baldwin, Jane, and Roberta Bolling Henry. *The Maryland Calendar of Wills: Wills from 1635 to 1685*. Vol. 1. Westminster, MD: Family Line Publications, 2007.

Billings, John Shaw. "Medical Reminiscences of the Civil War." *Transactions of the College of Physicians of Philadelphia*. Third series, vol. 27. Philadelphia, 1905.

Dammann, Gordon E., and Alfred Jay Bottet. "Images of Civil War Medicine." New York: Demos Health, 2007.

D.C. Recorder of Deeds. Land Records.

Emery, Fred A. "Mount Pleasant and Meridian Hill." *Records of the Columbia Historical Society* 33–34 (1932).

Garrison, Fielding, MD. *John Shaw Billings: A Memoir*. New York: G.P. Putnam's Sons, 1915.

Gates, Merrill E., ed. *Men of Mark in America: Ideals of American Life Told in Biographies of Eminent Living Americans*. Washington, D.C.: Men of Mark Publishing Company, 1906.

Goode, James M. *Best Addresses*. Washington, D.C.: Smithsonian Books, 2003.

Historic American Building Survey (HABS).

Historic American Engineering Record (HAER).

Horn, James. *Adapting to a New World: English Society in the Seventeenth-Century Chesapeake*. Chapel Hill: University of North Carolina Press, 1994.

Maryland Calendar of Wills. Vol. 1. Wills from 1635 to 1685.

Maryland Land Office Records.

McNeil, Priscilla. "Pretty Prospects: The History of a Land Grant." *Washington History* 14, no. 2 (2002–3).

———. "Rock Creek Hundred: Land Conveyed for the Federal City." *Washington History* 3, no. 1 (Spring/Summer 1991).

Mitchell, Mary. "Kalorama: Country Estate to Washington Mayfair." *Records of the Columbia Historical Society* 48 (1972):169–89.

Peden, Henry C. *Colonial Maryland Soldiers and Sailors: 1634–1734.* Westminster, MD: Willow Bend Books, 2001.

Prince George's County Land Records, 1717–26.

Proctor, John Clagett. "Beautiful Temple Heights Estate Is Center of Historic Washington Section." *Sunday Star*, September 22, 1940.

———. "Christian Hines, Author of 'Early Recollections of Washington City,' with Notes on the Hines Family." *Records of the Columbia Historical Society* 22 (1919).

———. "Indian Lore—The Legend of Widow's Mite." In *Washington, Past and Present: A History.* New York: Lewis Historical Publishing Company, Inc., 1930–1932.

Provine, Dorothy. *Compensated Emancipation in the District of Columbia, Petitions under the Act of April 16, 1862.* Westminster, MD: Heritage Books Inc., 2005.

Skordas, Gust, John M. Brewer and Arthur Trader. *The Early Settlers of Maryland; An Index to Names of Immigrants Compiled from Records of Land Patents, 1633–1680, in the Hall of Records, Annapolis, Maryland.* Hall of Records Commission. Baltimore, MD: Genealogical Pub. Co., 1968.

Slauson, Allan B., ed. *A History of the City of Washington: Its Men and Institutions.* Washington, D.C.: The Washington Post, 1903.

Streetcar and Bus Resources of Washington, D.C., 1862–1962. National Register of Historic Places Nomination. Washington, D.C.: National Park Service, 2006.

Thomas, Helen. *Front Row at the White House: My Life and Times.* New York: Simon and Schuster, 1999.

Washington Evening Star.

Washington Law Reporter, Vol. 42. District of Columbia. Supreme Court (1863–1936), District of Columbia. Court of Appeals, United States. Court of Appeals (District of Columbia Circuit).

Washington Post.

INDEX

ABOUT THE AUTHOR

Stephen A. Hansen has lived in Kalorama Triangle for over twenty-five years. He works as a historic preservation consultant and is principal of D.C. Historic Designs, LLC, a historic preservation and architectural design company. Previously, he worked for the National Park Service and as a historical archaeologist in the region. He is a member of the Historical Society of Washington, AIA-DC and the Kalorama Citizens Association and has served on the boards of several historic preservation organizations. He is a graduate of Oberlin College, The George Washington University and Goucher College. Stephen lives in Truesdell's Addition to Washington Heights subdivision in Kalorama Triangle.